EFFECT OF PSYCHOSOCIAL WORK ENVIRONMENT ON JOB BURNOUT AND TURNOVER INTENTION AMONG RETAIL TEXTILE SHOP SALESPERSONS IN KERALA

Ms. RAKHY K S

Acknowledgement

This thesis remained on track and was completed with the encouragement and support of my mentors, family, well-wishers, and friends. At the end of my thesis, it is a pleasure to express my heartfelt appreciation to everyone who contributed in numerous ways to the success of this study and made it an unforgettable experience for me.

To begin with, I would like to express my gratitude to **Mata Amritanandamayi Devi,** Chancellor of Amrita Vishwa Vidyapeetham, for providing me with the opportunity to pursue a Ph.D. at this prestigious institution. I am indebted to **Swami Poornamritananda Puri** for bestowing his blessings on me to complete my research successfully.

I would like to acknowledge my indebtedness and render my warmest thanks to my supervisor, **Dr. A.S. Ambily,** Assistant Professor (S.G) and Head of the Department, Department of Commerce and Management, Amrita School of Arts, Humanities, and Commerce for providing me with valuable support and motivation. Her dynamism, vision, sincerity, and motivation have deeply inspired me, and it was a great privilege and honour to work and study under her guidance.

Thank you to my doctoral committee members, **Dr. U. Krishnakumar,** Director & Research Supervisor in the Department of Computer Science and I.T., Amrita School of Arts, Humanities, and Commerce and **Dr. P. P. Vijayalakshmi**, Professor and Research Supervisor (Member, Board of Studies in English Language and Literature) at the Department of English and Languages, Amrita School of Arts, Humanities, and Commerce.

I gratefully acknowledge **Dr. N. Ajith Kumar**,was always approachable for any help required. In addition, I am indebted to **Dr. Devi Sowmyaja**, Assistant Professor, School of Management Studies, CUSAT, for providing expert guidance for completing my research.

The thesis has also benefited from the comments and suggestions made by **Dr. Vidhya Vinayachandran**, Assistant Professor, Department of Commerce and

Management, Amrita School of Arts, Humanities, and Commerce. I would like to give a special thanks to **Dr. Prasanth A P**, Assistant Professor, Department of Commerce and management Amrita School of Arts, Humanities, and Commerce, for all the support and fruitful suggestions.

Many thanks to **Dr. N.V Sreedharan,** Professor, Department of Commerce and Management, Amrita School of Arts, Humanities, and Commerce, for all department-level support. In addition, I am highly indebted to my former research supervisor **Dr. Sony Vijayan**. My respectful thanks to **Dr. M.G. Priya** (PGP Chair), Amrita School of Arts, Humanities, and Commerce.

I would like to convey my heartfelt gratitude to all the teaching and non-teaching staff, at Amrita School of Arts, Humanities, and Commerce for their support. I wish to express my sense of gratitude to the library staff of Amrita School of Arts and Science, Kochi, who helped me a lot in availing of relevant literature.

My sincere thanks to **Mr. Sathyaraj T.L,** Assistant Labour Officer, Thiruvananthapuram, for his constant help in getting data collection permission from retail textile shops. I am highly thankful that **P. Viji,** the women's union leader, 'Asanghaditha Mekhala Thozhilali Union' (Union for workers of unorganised sectors) as a women's group 'Penkoottu', in Kerala for her valuable suggestions.

A thank you would be a very simple expression to show my gratitude and appreciation to **Mr. Bright Singh**, my beloved uncle, who helped me get permission from retailers for the survey. Special thanks to my aunts **Mrs. Beena B.S and Mrs. Beena P.K** for the overwhelming support throughout my research.

I would like to thank my friend **Dr. Bessy D'cruz** (Research Associate at Kuwait University), and my brothers **Sanker T. Gopal** (University of Portsmouth, United Kingdom) and **Vishnu T. Gopal** (Ecole Nationale de l'aviation civile, Toulouse University) for their whole-hearted cooperation, and help to gather necessary research articles. Special word of thanks to **Mrs. Shiny Thyagarajan** (Assistant Professor, Avila College of Education) for her help and support.

My heartfelt thanks to all salespersons, especially **Mr. Rahul R, Mr. Jyothish, and Mr. Sasi Kumar,** who gave their time and were a great help in bringing in other participants to the study.

I deeply regard the support of my friends **Dr. Elsa Elizabeth Jacob, Dr. Devi Sekar, Dr. Ann Mary Jones, Dr. Veena M. Dr. Pleasa Serin Abraham, and Ms. Anusree M.** for being with me and helping in all possible ways. A special thank you to my friend **Ms. Nisha Sreekumar** for constantly motivating me, helping me prepare the chapters, and being available whenever I needed moral support.

I am grateful to my husband, **Mr. Rex S.**, for his support, love, and extreme cooperation at every stage to make this research endeavor a resounding success. I truly acknowledge my parents-in-law, **Mrs. Saroja S.** and **Mr. Suresh Babu P.,** whose support made me proceed in this direction smoothly. Their sacrifice had no bounds when it concerned freeing me from my responsibilities and duties, which helped me focus on my work. I am also thankful to my children, **Reya Rex,** and **Rithika Rex,** for taking care of their studies and examinations in my absence.

I am thankful to my parents, **Mr. K.G Soman** and **Mrs. P.K Balamoneyamma,** for their immense support, love, and encouragement while the research work was in progress.

Numerous thanks to my respondents for their help and transparency during my research.

Last but not least, I thank Almighty for making me feel His ever-pervading presence in all my ups and downs of research. I prostrate before Him and submit my success in all humility to His Grace and Blessings

RAKHY K.S

Contents

Chapter 4
Data Analysis & Discussion

CHAPTER 1

INTRODUCTION TO THE STUDY

The first section of this chapter contains a Background of the Research, an outline of the Retail Textile Sector, Retail Textile Sector in India, Kerala Scenario in Textile Retailing, Salespersons in the Retail Textile Shops, Research Gap Identified through a Review of Literature, Research Questions employed, Research Objectives, Problem Statements, Significance of the study, and the second section consists of Research Methodology which comprises Research Design of the Study, Sampling Methods, the Population of the Study, Variables and Measurement Scales, Scope and Limitations of the study, and the Thesis' Chapter Scheme.

1.1 Background of the Study

The world's economic structure has shifted from manufacturing to service in the latter part of the twentieth century (EU-OSHA, 2014). Till the turn of the twenty-first century, the phrase "healthy organisation" was used to refer to a business's financial stability. Nowadays, a healthy workplace is viewed as composite well-being of various physiological, psychological, and social factors (Bowen & Ford, 2002). Work has changed over time, and the demands placed on workers have changed due to this shift in nature. As a result, the emotional and psychological strain has increased, while physical efforts have dropped or remained unchanged (Marmot et al., 1999; de Jonge et al.,1999). Even though mental and emotional difficulties exist in the manufacturing industry, they are not given much attention. (Hammer et al.,2004).

Having a job is usually necessary for maintaining a stable income and socio-economic status. Apart from economic survival, a person's employment is essential for socialisation. It gives opportunities for individual progress and development, and a positive self-image is a critical social function that enables engagement in social networks beyond primary groups. Work and life are influenced by various circumstances, including the physical, social, psychological, political, and economic environment (Goetzel et al.,2002).

With the growth of positive psychology, scholars have begun to consider the welfare of employees at work. (Seligman & Csikszentmihalyi, 2000; Huhtala & Parzefall, 2007; Danna&Griffin, 1999). An individual's happiness at work should be measured in terms of job satisfaction, satisfaction with a co-worker and other work-related factors.

The psychosocial work environment, which combines psychological and social aspects of the workplace, is gaining popularity. Psychosocial work demands, job control, effort and reward, excessive workloads, emotional pressure, autonomy, and social support from bosses or co-workers contribute to the Psychosocial Work Environment.

Significant changes in the global market and its related demands and opportunities led to a competitive market. In addition, as a new method of work culture, new technologies, processes, products, and a more varied workforce resulted in a more intense, irregular, unpredictable, and insecure job emerged as a result of this (Houtman et al., 2016; Dollard et al., 2007).

The working population was confronted with increased physical and emotional demands to adjust to this new reality. Additionally, this created several difficulties when the psychosocial resources were not addressed effectively (Bakker & Demerouti, 2007). There is much scientific evidence demonstrating psychosocial risks in the workplace and their detrimental effects on worker health (Bonde,2008; Wieclaw et al.,2008). They arise due to inefficient work design, poor management, and organisational and social context (Stansfield & Candy, 2006).

Workers in the European Union have reported being exposed to psychosocial risk on the job, which has serious consequences for workers, workplaces, and society (Milczarek et al., 2012). For example, according to a 2012-14 United Kingdom labour strength study, the total number of cases of job-related anxiety, depression and stress is estimated to be 39 per cent, and approximately 24 per cent of healthcare workers report being bullied or harassed by co-workers.

According to the Austrian employee health monitor from 2009, 42 per cent of managerial workers leave their job early, owing to work-related psychological issues. Low mental health and psychosocial risks at work have a substantial economic impact on the Austrian workforce. Over the last ten years, the average cost of psychological hazards claims has continuously climbed, and they currently account for the highest average cost of all reimbursement claims. Per year 7820 Austrian workers receive compensation for work-related psychosocial disorders. (Banco Europeo de reconstrucción y Desarrollo, 2015).

"Abusive supervision" is reported to be a prevalent organisational threat in the United States, costing $23.8 billion yearly in expenditure. This has decreased efficiency, reduced morale, higher absenteeism, and workplace departure (Pradhan and Jena,2017). It is estimated that 27 per cent of American employees are subjected to "abusive behaviour" at work at some point of time in their careers. In 2010, bullying and harassment were observed to be 9.5 per cent in French workplaces, increasing to 12.9 per cent in 2020. In New Zealand, 15 per cent of 800 employees from managerial and non-managerial levels reported being bullied. Power harassment was reported by almost 45 per cent of a representative sample from Japanese organisations. In addition, 14 to 20 per cent of employees from selected universities in Japan said they were subjected to cyberbullying by web ports, e-mail, and text messages at least once a week (ILO, 2020).

These negative repercussions affect employees' physical and psychological well-being (HaSPA, 2012). Continuous involvement in this type of stressors can result in Burnout (Maslach & Leiter, 2008; Schaufeli & Greenglass, 2001). Job burnout is chronic stress, and if it is not successfully managed, it leads to three categories of symptoms, involving state of "Physical, Emotional, and Mental Exhaustion" (Pines, Neal, Hammer & Icekson, 2011). So Emotional, Mental and Physical Exhaustion are the main challenges with Job Burnout. Moreover, Burnout results in decreased productivity and effectiveness for those who remain on the job. As a result, it is linked to decreasing commitment and diminished job satisfaction to the job or organisation (Maslach and Leiter, 2008). Burnout is a subjective experience that is context-dependent. However, new research indicates that Burnout can be hazardous to the workforce, affecting employees' attitudes and behaviours (Weigl et al., 2016).

Burnout is significant for both the individual and the workplace since it is associated with critical consequences. Burnout has been linked to various occupation withdrawal behaviours such as absenteeism, intention to quit, and actual turnover.

Increased risk of Burnout, is linked to a higher likelihood of leaving the organisation. Therefore, employee turnover intention can be defined as a psychological response to a specific organisational environment that manifests through various organisational withdrawal behaviours, ranging from intention to quit to leaving the organisation (Kraut, 1975).

Individuals plan turnover decisions in a more or less predictable order over a succession of phases (Steel, 2002). Therefore, if Burnout is not averted, it can result in a loss of productivity in the workplace, morale decline, and poor psychological or physical health (Pienaar & Willemse, 2008). The term "employee turnover intention" refers to an "employee's tendency to leave the job for which he or she is currently employed" (Ngamkroeckjoti, Ounprechavanit, &Kijboonchoo., 2012).

Regardless of its location, size, or business nature, every organisation is always concerned about employees' quitting intentions (Long. et al., 2012). Consequently, Turnover Intention is a significant predictor of actual turnover. However, it is costly for organisations because it entails significant costs associated with recruiting new employees by providing induction and training programmes even though the loss of a skilled employee may never be compensated (Aladwan et al., 2013).

This phenomenon is relevant in the retail sector because psychosocial problems remain prevalent in the retail sector (Stansfeld & Candy, 2006). In addition, the retail industry is rapidly expanding throughout the world, contributing significantly to the global economy's expansion (Menguc et al., 2017). As retail businesses expand, competition becomes more intense, and businesses increasingly rely on superior service for acquiring and retaining customers.

The general retailing industry has undergone significant transformation in recent years, most notably in textile retailing, which was previously a made-to-order market for clothing but has evolved into a ready-to-wear market.

1.2 An Overview of the Retail Textile Sector

The business of obtaining apparel from manufacturers and reselling it to customers is known as retailing. In order to sell products, marketing is utilised at both the wholesale and retail levels. Companies that do not sell their items at retail must sell their products at wholesale prices to retailers such as boutiques, branded stores, privately owned shops, and internet sales companies (Newman &Cullen,2002).

The apparel and fashion industry comprises a diverse range of garments. Clothing for children, men, boys, women, and girls are the broad categories the industry is split. Demand for the industry is expected to increase in the coming years due to favourable demographics, rising per capita income, and a shift in consumer preference toward branded products (Rashid & Barnes,2021).

Due to the fierce competition, clothing companies frequently create alliances to present a more formidable front. In addition, successful advertising techniques and a focus on niche markets aid garment manufacturers in producing various designs to make retailers more revenue (Mccormick et al., 2014).

The global garment market is propelled forward by a growing population, increased urbanisation, and a shift in global economic power.With the considerable expansion in the Asia-Pacific region, the market is expected to grow at a rate of 4.8 per cent between 2020 and 2025, reaching $ 2,006.4 billion.

The global fashion retail sector is very competitive, dominated by a small number of giant corporates such as Inditex and Nike. Other large corporations such as H&M, Adidas and Gap Inc, and Zara and Inditex account for only eight per cent of the market share (Fibre to Fashion,2019).

Figure 1.1

Global Apparel Market Size 2012-2025

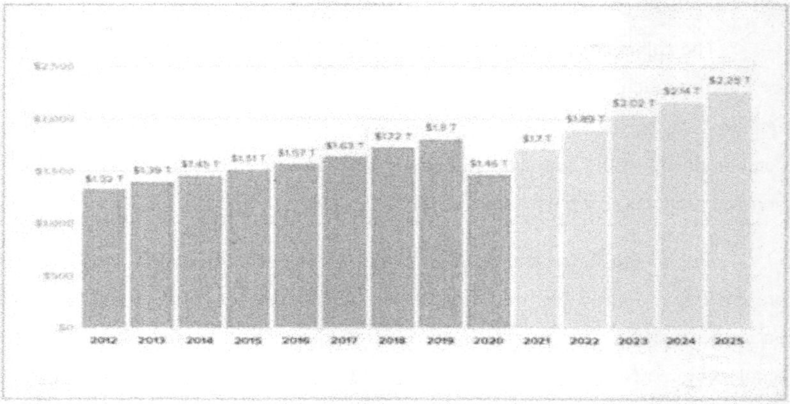

***Note*:** This figure represents the Global Apparel Market Size from 2012-2025

The worldwide apparel market was valued at $1.46 trillion in 2020, representing a decrease of nearly 20 per cent from the previous year. It is expected to rebound in the coming years, reaching $1.84 billion. - As a result of the COVID-19 pandemic, the apparel industry's loss was $342 billion in 2020 compared to 2019. Globally, the apparel industry employs an estimated 75 million people, including textile manufacturers, designers, sewers, tailors, retailers, and a variety of other occupations and businesses (Merritt,2020)

The Asia Pacific region is the world's major clothing market, accounting for 33 per cent of total global demand in the apparel industry. Western Europe comes in second place, which is 28 per cent of the global apparel market. The smallest share of global apparel demand at one per cent is from Africa.

Globally, women's apparel was the most popular category in 2021, with sales reaching $165 billion. According to industry estimates, consumers today purchase approximately 400 per cent more clothing than they did just 20 years ago. This modern industry is characterised by short product life cycles, extensive product differentiation, and rapid consumer demand changes (Clare,2018).

Every year, more than 80 billion new pieces of clothing are purchased worldwide. Unfortunately, with the introduction of new clothing into our lives, consumers discard their old clothing at an alarming rate. Clothing has traditionally been something that people have held onto for an extended period, but this is no longer the case with cheap clothing now readily available.

Fashion spending, on the other hand, is not equally distributed. In terms of individual apparel and footwear sales, China continues to be the world's largest market ($380 billion), followed by the United States ($370 billion).

The global apparel market is fragmented, with several major and minor players competing for customer attention. The unorganised market in developing countries is large and diverse, offering consumers diverse products. Even though the extensive distribution networks of global brands significantly impact international markets, they are subjected to intense competition from local manufacturers regarding regional fashion preferences and pricing (Report linker,2021).

1.3 Retail Textile Sector in India

The Indian retail sector is undergoing a major transformation. In India, retailing is slowly but steadily becoming the country's next boom industry and growing at the fastest rate. Consumer purchasing patterns and behaviour are changing consistently. The expansion of India's retail sector is restricted to urban areas and are also gaining ground in rural areas (Grosso et al., 2018).

As predicted, apparel sales rose in India at $71 billion;It is now the fifth-largest, knocking the UK into sixth place. The industry consists of large, medium, and small players like Kirana shops and mom-and-pop stores. Amongst the prominent players include Lifestyle and Reliance Retail Pantaloons, Trent Retail, Reliance Retail, Shopper's Stop, The Arvind group, Madura Fashion, Raymond Apparel and the Future Group, on the other hand, have all launched their own fashion labels in the country (IBEF,2021).

In this era of globalisation, India is perceived as the next country with the greatest 'Growth Potential' after China, owing to the low cost of its labour and natural resources. Over the years, India has also established itself as one of the most appealing market destinations for apparel retailers worldwide. With annual growth rates ranging from 12-15 per cent, apparel is the second most popular retail category in India after food and beverages. In the coming years, it is expected to take the lead in the country's organised retail sector, according to analysts

As their income increase, consumers in India are spending more and experimenting with a wider range of products, brands, and categories. Rather than being solely functional, apparel has evolved into a category that conveys appearance, prestige, and image. Consumers are looking for clothing that is both reasonably priced and fashionable. The expansion of modern trade has contributed to an increase in the demand for branded and value apparel. This, combined with the emergence of new industries and professional job opportunities, has also contributed to the increase in demand for office wear. More than half of India's population is under the age of 25. Young Indians are aspirational, demanding, and concerned with finding fashionable and affordable clothing at a reasonable price. Clothing has a ten-per cent market share in the organised retail category at the moment (Vikash,2022).

The apparel retail industry in India has undergone a significant transformation in recent years, with the introduction of new formats as well as the adoption of global concepts and constructs, notwithstanding modifications to suit the Indian culture. Not only does it provide a wide range of options for Indian consumers, but it also represents a significant increase in employment opportunities for people with a wide range of skill sets.

Clothing stores can be found in abundance in Indian cities and towns, particularly in shopping malls and markets. According to industry experts, the total apparel market in India is worth between ₹ 48,000 and ₹ 50,000 crore per annum. However, only ₹ 9000-10,000 crores are spent on branded apparel out of the total amount spent.

Figure 1.2

Major Apparel Countries by Sales Value from 2019-2024

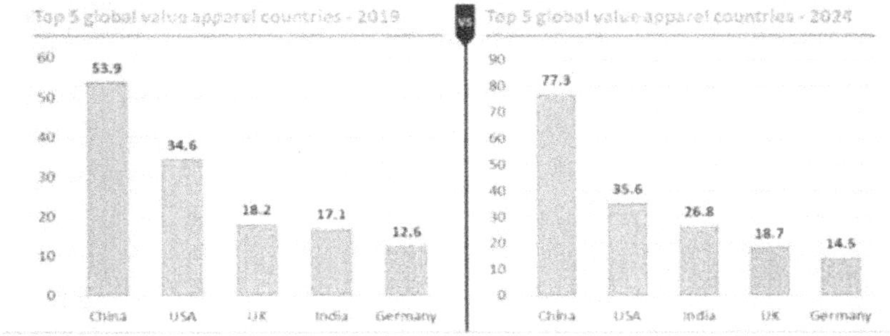

Note: Global Data Apparel Intelligencer

1.4 Kerala Scenario in Textile Retailing

Numerous retail textile shops can be found throughout Kerala's urban, semi-urban, and rural areas, particularly in shopping malls and markets. In Kerala, textile retailing units can be broadly classified into two types, namely 'government and private. The former category includes units owned or supported by the National Textile Corporation, the Kerala State Handloom Development Corporation (Handveev), the Kerala State Handloom Weavers Cooperative Society (Hantex), the Tamil Nadu Handloom Weavers Cooperative Society (Co-optex), and the Khadi and Village Industries Board (KVIB).

These shops are again classified as 'organised' or 'unorganised' based on their organisational structure. The organised retailing units include general textile shops, exclusive showrooms, franchises, and select stores, while the unorganised retailing units primarily consist of door-to-door vendors. Thus, it is appropriate to emphasise Kerala is well-served by a network of textile outlets catering to end-users. As per the latest report from the concerned labour department, 14,606 textile shops in Kerala are registered under Kerala Shops and Commercial Establishment Act,1960. Moreover, a total of 71267 employees work as a salesperson.

Both small and large players dominate Kerala's retail textile market. There are a variety of stores, both traditional and modern. Traditional outlets are family-owned businesses that are typically small and cramped, with little emphasis on attractive displays and rely on word of mouth or a strong customer relationship for advertising. They carry a small selection of unbranded or locally made and popular items.

On the other hand, modern clothing stores are auspicious, with attractive window displays. Leading domestic retailers are consolidating their positions by increasing and stabilising their operational scale, logistics and technology initiatives. Additionally, a few significant foreign players have sold their branded apparel in Kerala for many years (Nair & Nair,2018).

Kerala alone has more than 50,000 square feet of retail space, which is more than all of the national stores of Central, Lifestyle, and Shoppers Stop combined. In addition, the Kalyan Silks megastore in Chennai and the Kalyan Silks megastore in Ernakulam do more than Rs 150 crore in annual sales. Moreover, Kalyan Silk operates 85,000 square-foot showrooms in Thrissur. Furthermore, they have nine more spacious outlets in different parts of Kerala (Talwar,2010).

"Seematti" is another one-stop shop for customers. Seematti has been involved in the fashion industry for more than a hundred years. Seematti has a five lakh square feet floor, including facility and utility areas. This retail chain even made it into the Guinness world record and Limca books of records to create the world's largest hand-woven silk saree (500 metres long).

Jayalakshmi silks is yet another well-known retail establishment in Kerala, with four showrooms located in the state's major cities: Cochin, Trivandrum, Calicut, and Thrissur.

Other major textile shops in Kerala include Aiyappas, Chennai Silks, Pothys, Seemas, Kasavukendra, and Parthas, which sell a wide variety of ready-made dresses, sarees, churidar materials, children's, men's and women's, party and fashion wear, Kancheepuram silk sarees, traditional Kerala dresses, and other items.

1.5 Salespersons in the Retail Textile Shops

Over the last decade, Kerala's textile retail shops have transformed their image more than expected. The prime importance of the current retail textile shop is consumer support and retail service based on consumers' desires. So, retail management continuously monitors consumer demands and other factors influencing purchasing behaviour (Sharma, 2001).

The workforce as salespersons has numerous opportunities in the retail industry. Salespersons are the face of retail establishments. Frontline employees' service is essential to maintaining quality, retaining consumer satisfaction, and achieving organisational goals. Customer service representatives are typically exposed to various interpersonal stressors, including lack of support from co-workers, lack of recognition from managers and customer incivility. They are underpaid, untrained, and overworked (Witt & Gross, 2020).

Typically, once an item is sold from shops, the retailer ensures that it is according to the trends. It is gradually replaced by new designs, styles, and colours. The importance of the store layout and decor cannot be understated. Frequent customer appreciates changes in the layout; otherwise, they may get the impression that the store's inventory is stagnant. Category management becomes critical as transforming the design into production and delivery must be completed before the market's fashion changes. Without a doubt, the most critical factor in determining a retailer's success is the appeal and quality of the products it stocks. Indeed, another factor contributing to success is the salesperson's attentiveness and knowledge. Unfortunately, these factors combine to create multiple stressors for salespersons, particularly in retail stores (Low,2001).

Customers are regarded as a "second manager" in retail trade, and they have greater control over their preferences and domination than the salesperson. A salesperson is an individual whose primary responsibility is to create positive relationships with the customer to achieve organisational objectives (Chung et al., 2012). The role of a boundary spanner is to bridge the gap between an organisation and its customers. Salespersons should emit positive and friendly emotions to increase customer loyalty and improve service quality. When working in a "dog eats dog" setting, the salesperson is subjected to much pressure from superiors to provide better service quality (Singh, 2014).

Consistent research indicates that psychosocial issues are more prevalent among service sector employees. Prolonged exposure to these stressors results in emotional exhaustion, mental disorders, decreased quality of life, absenteeism, and intention to leave (Singh, Goolsby, & Rhoads, 1994).

The Indian workplace is undergoing rapid changes due to the country's economic conditions, technological advancements, corporate employment policies, and demographic trends. Additionally, we are experiencing rapid global economic growth, which has resulted in a slew of potentially serious issues, including environmental and occupational hazards, workplace safety, compensation, and psychosocial stress (Saiyed & Tiwari, 2004).

A new work culture emerged as a result of globalisation. As a result, work became more precarious. New technological innovations, blurred lines between work and leisure time, and increased demands for learning and acquiring new skills. Pressure to increase productivity, job insecurity, reduced benefits, and less time for socialising with co-workers deteriorated the work-life balance also. They have been forced to suppress their emotions towards rude customers to maintain service quality. Globalisation, outsourcing, technological innovations, new types of work, and dynamic employment trends influenced India's industrial climate (Houtman et al., 2016).

So, retailers must understand how to increase employee satisfaction with jobs (Booth & Hamer, 2006; Arndt et al., 2006) and make them stay in retail careers by maintaining a good Psychosocial Work Environment (Kim et al., 2009). Retailers can become more competitive in the market by lowering recruiting and training costs, maintaining a good work environment, and providing greater value to customers,

In this context, the research covered the most distressing and perplexing issues faced by a salesperson in retail textile shops, including their Psychosocial Work Environment, Job Burnout, and Turnover Intention.

1.6 Research Gap Identified

The psychosocial workplace is a multidimensional construct studied from epidemiological to developmental perspectives (Sharma, 2011). Many studies in Western countries exist on the Psychosocial Work Environment, Job Burnout, and Turnover Intention perspectives. This growing awareness of the need for action is reflected in an increased focus on psychosocial hazards and work-related stress at the international, regional, and national levels, through assessment and management to the development of legislation, strategies, policies, the dissemination of information, awareness-raising campaigns, proliferation of research networks and professional associations.

Because of these intensive campaigns, employees and employers are aware of the antecedents and consequences of psychosocial risk factors in the workplace and try to prevent them to maintain a positive and productive work environment.

Awareness of the importance of a good psychosocial work environment lacking in most low- and middle-income countries. In India retail market is as old as in the global context. However, the concept of organized retailing is comparatively new. Hence academic literature on psychosocial risk factors of salespersons in the retail sector in India is lacking in comparison to western countries. However, certain specialised cross-sectional studies of the Indian labour market, particularly in the service sector, such as education, health care, call centres, and IT sector have been carried out.

According to LinkedIn research, about 41% of Indian professionals believe job and income insecurity are the greatest mental health hazards. In addition, customer incivility hurts the emotional exhaustion and service recovery performance of Indian frontline banking personnel (Zahoor& Siddiqi, 2021).

Burnout is highly prevalent among Indian healthcare professionals, with close to one-fourth of them suffering from burnout. A number of personal and professional factors like excessive stress, lack of satisfaction, and a feeling of being overworked are associated with burnout (Kesarwani, Husaain& George)

The study was conducted among call centre workers, to assess the relationship between work-related musculoskeletal disorders and workplace psychological stress.

Statistical analysis showed a significant association between the prevalence of musculoskeletal disorders and occupational mental stress (Nafeesa et al.).

A cross-sectional study by, Shenoi, Kalyanaraman, Pillai, Raghava and Day (2018) evaluated the association between psychological distress and symptoms of burnout among physicians. They reported that Burnout syndrome was high among pediatric physicians. They also found a positive correlation between psychological distress and symptoms of burnout among the total sample.

All these studies show that based on the nature of work, psychosocial risk factors also vary in the Indian workplace. So, it is relevant to study what are the most influencing psychosocial risks factors among salespersons and it will be helpful for retailers to prevent job burnout and turnover intention.

In India exists an excellent market potential for the retail industry because of the peculiar socio-economic and demographic profile of the very vast Indian population. To be effective in the twenty-first century, retail businesses must attract, recruit, and retain skilled salespersons (Rhoads et al., 2002).

Salespersons have a critical role in providing excellent service and retaining consumers. However, salespersons, particularly in retail stores, operate in a stressful environment frequently connected with complaints and frustrations about bad client behaviour, bullying by employees, abusive supervisors, long working hours and prolonged standing, job uncertainty, and low pay (Singh, 2014).

Decades of research, depict that salesperson turnover continues to be a significant issue in India's retail industry. A high turnover rate impairs an organization's efficiency. When organizations lose knowledgeable and experienced personnel.

But existing studies still lack a detailed explanation of the effect of psychosocial work environment on the turnover intention with mediating effect of job burnout in the Indian retail textile sector.

The findings of this study will help textile retailers to identify the major psychosocial risk factors which lead to salespersons' job burnout and turnover intention.

Thus, this study would be relevant considering the growing problem of the Psychosocial Work Environment related to retail textile shops and also helps to understand the importance of maintaining salespersons' physical, emotional, and mental health to avoid Job Burnout and turnover intention issues. The research gaps identified from the literature have been described in detail in chapter two.

1.7 Problem Statements

The study was initially motivated by observations and informal discussions with a few experts in the retail textile sector and trade union leaders. After that, the researcher looked at various literature and studies that had already been done. Local and national newspaper reports were also referred to regarding this issue.

After receiving a complaint alleging that the human rights of the retail textile salesperson in Kerala are being violated, the National Human Rights Commission issued a notice to the Kerala government, requesting reports on the matter. Based on those reports, salespersons are allegedly not allowed to sit or use the restroom during their more than ten-hour shifts (Himanshi,2016).

In Kerala, the working condition of the salespersons in the textile sales sector are deplorable and are subject to rampant exploitation. Even laws are constantly being violated (Smithan,2019). Salespersons are frequently denied breaks and are dismissed for silly reasons (Aabha,2016). Some research reports indicate that salespersons employed in retail textile shops act as mannequins to generate more business in today's competitive market. Additionally, they are employed to enhance the attractiveness of the businesses and are required to stand as mannequins throughout the working hours. (Muyarath & Roopak.,2018).

There is a dearth of empirical studies in the retail textile sector in India to understand the effect of the Psychosocial Work Environment on Job Burnout and Turnover Intention. Retailers provide centralised air-conditioned showrooms, car parking, elevators, and individual customer services to attract more customers. At the same time, these retailers are not much concerned about the well-being of their salespersons. Furthermore, most retail textile shops are locally owned and lack of well-defined employee management systems to promote the Psychosocial Work Environment.

As a result, most salespersons are underpaid, overworked, and highly stressed. They have high job demands, less social support, less job control, are required to work for long and extra hours, and always work at weekends and evenings. Moreover, all these ineffective retail employee management systems negatively influence the salespersons' emotional, mental, and physical well-being at the workplace.

With the liberalisation of the retail sector, Indian corporations, privately-owned big retailers, and foreign retailers entered the market, and modern retail evolved. Simultaneously, the nature and status of employment have also changed (Reardon &Gulati, 2008). Most of these retail salespersons now receive social security benefits like employees' state insurance schemes, provident funds, and many other benefits from their concerned labour welfare fund board.

In modern retailing, expectations from salespersons have also increased. Salespersons must be skilful. Skills include interacting nicely with customers, acting according to the needs and wants of the customers, helping them select their suitable product, and salespersons must have good product knowledge.

Due to acute competition in the retail sector, retailers always insist that salespersons keep their service quality at its maximum Salespersons have to act as a boundary spanner. They also have to act according to the needs and wants of the customers and achieve the organisational goals. It creates multiple stress among salespersons. Retail salespersons have to work late evenings, weekends, and holidays. Because of the nature of their job, they have to stand for a long time. This prolonged standing creates various health issues. Maybe because of all these factors turnover rate is very high in the Indian retail sector.

This study analyses whether the Psychosocial Work Environment and Job Burnout have influenced salespersons' Turnover Intention. Moreover, because of the intense competition between retailers, it is crucial to maintain the service quality to the customer's needs. As a result, the psychosocial well-being of a salesperson is vital in the retail environment. (Sharma, 2001).

1.7 Significance of the Study

Despite decades of research, salesperson turnover continues to be a significant issue in India's retail industry. A high turnover rate impairs an organisation's efficiency. When organisations lose knowledgeable and experienced personnel, they suffer.

In retail establishments, salespersons play a vital role in creating the consumer–retailer relationship. The consumer forms an impression of the salespersons early in their interaction (Ambady et al., 2006). As a result, salespersons in retail textile shops determine the shops' sales. They are an essential asset to the shop since they project its image to the customer. However, with fierce competition among retailers for customer retention, businesses must alter their retail service for customer satisfaction, wherein retail salesperson's play a vital role (Sharma, 2001).

This study can help identify psychosocial risk factors and reduce them to avoid salesperson turnover. The study's result can help retailers understand the importance of maintaining salespersons' physical, emotional, and mental health to avoid Job Burnout issues among salespersons. This study becomes imperative for employers to initiate strategies to lower turnover frequency. This study can help employers in the retail textiles sector widen their efforts towards increasing their employees' recognition and social support.

This study may provide new insights into specific salespersons' support and care dimensions that substantially impact psychosocial well-being.

1.8 Research Questions

The research questions narrow down the purpose statement. Typically, researchers develop the research questions before determining the study's methods.

Research Question 1: Does the Psychosocial Work Environment have any effect on Retail Textile Salespersons Turnover Intention?

Research Question 2: Does the Retail Textile Psychosocial Work Environment Influence Salespersons' Job Burnout?

Research Question 3: Does the Psychosocial Work Environment and Job Burnout influence Salespersons' Turnover Intention?

Research Question 4: Is there any Mediating Role of Job Burnout on the relationship between Psychosocial Work Environment and Salespersons' Turnover Intention?

1.9Objectives of the Study

1. To study the effect of Psychosocial Work Environment on Turnover Intention
2. To study the effect of Psychosocial Work Environment on Job Burnout
3. To examine the effect of Job Burnout on Turnover Intention
4. To examine the mediating effect of Job Burnout on Psychosocial Work Environment and Turnover Intention

1.11. Hypotheses of the Study

Hypotheses used in research enable the researcher to summarise the findings to operationalise the variables. Research Hypotheses or assumptions are statements in quantitative research in which the investigator makes a hypothetical prediction or speculation about the outcome of an association among attributes (Creswell, 2012). The research questions and hypotheses guide the researcher since it is survey research with cross-sectional techniques using structured questionnaires and pilot-tested instrumentation. The research hypotheses are stated in the following way:

H1: Psychosocial Work Environment has a significant influence on Turnover Intention

H2: Psychosocial Work Environment has a significant influence on Job Burnout

H3: Job Burnout has a significant influence on Turnover Intention

H4: Job Burnout has mediating effect on the relationship between Psychosocial Work Environment and Turnover Intention

1.12 Research Methodology

1.12.1 Research Design of the Study

Arranging the data collection and analysis settings to maximise relevance to the study purpose is known as a research design. It is a research framework for conducting research and establishes data gathering, measurement, and analysis. It describes the techniques for acquiring data necessary to structure or solve research challenges (Selltiz et al., 1981).

This study is descriptive as it focuses on collecting primary data, analysing and confirming the conceptual framework, presenting the study's findings, making explanations, and giving conclusions. It is based on cross-sectional and quantitative research with data collected through a questionnaire deploying an interview schedule. The opinions have been measured at one point in time from each respondent.

Table 1.1

Process of Research Design

First Phase	Determination of the variables that are to be utilised in the research investigation and constructing a tool validation procedure
Second Phase	Identification of the population sample, elicitation of information
Third Phase	Analyse data using suitable statistical procedures, and report writing

1.12.1 Sampling Methods

Sampling is part of the study design. The sampling process comprises several fundamental problems, such as how to take a sample, process it, what kind of sample to take, how big it should be, and how to regulate and adjust for response errors (Malhotra & Dash, 2011). A well-thought-out sample plan and design were used to obtain sufficient replies.

1.12.2 The Population of the Study

The study population is the set of objects from which inferences are to be drawn. Since this research involved the effect of the psychosocial work environment on job burnout and turnover intention among retail textile salespersons in Kerala, the target population for the study was the salespersons in big retail textile shops registered under the Kerala Shops and Commercial Establishments Act 1960.

1.12.3 Sampling Unit

The sampling unit of this study is a salesperson working in a big retail textile shop in Kerala.

Salespersons were sourced across the three selected districts in Kerala. Justification for selecting three districts is provided in section 1.11.6.

1.12.4 Selection of Sampling Technique

Choosing a sample strategy includes a broader nature of decisions (Malhotra & Dash, 2011). There are two sorts of sampling techniques: probability sampling and non-probability sampling. Probability sampling is also referred to as random or chance sampling. Nonprobability sampling is a technique that provides no basis for each item in the population's likelihood of being included in the sample (Kothari, 2011).

A well-considered sample plan and design were used to ensure that feasible responses were obtained. The present study utilised multi-stage random sampling for selecting the districts. In Kerala, Trivandrum, Ernakulam, and Calicut have the highest number of salespersons working in retail textile shops. So, these districts were selected for the sampling. The total number of salespersons working in registered retail textile shops is procured from the respective labour commission office. The sampling design best suited for this study was the probability sampling method. Among probability sampling techniques, the researcher has chosen multi-stage random sampling.

1.12.5 Determining the Sampling Frame

A sampling framework is a way of showing the population to which the study group belongs. It comprises a set of directions for recognising the target population (Malhotra & Dash, 2011). It was not logical for the researcher to cover the all the registered retail textile shops in Kerala. Therefore, geographical constraints mandated that the study to be limited only a selected number of districts. So, with the help of multi-stage random sampling techniques researcher has formulated the sampling frame.

In the first stage of the multi-stage random sampling, the researcher has collected data about the total population of salespersons working in big retail textile shops in Kerala from the labour commission office, Trivandrum. In the second stage, based on the total population in the big retail textile shops, the geographical areas of Kerala were divided into three zone, the south zone, the central zone, and the north zone. Then, the third stage selected one district from each zone based on the highest number of salespersons' population. Thus, the Calicut district has the highest number of salespersons working in big retail textile shops in the north zone. The Ernakulam district from the central zone has the highest number of salespersons in big retail textile shops. Finally, the Trivandrum district was selected from the south zone.

The labour department divided districts into different circles according to the number of shops, each circle being administered by a different labour officer. Trivandrum is divided into eight circles, each of which is headed by eight labour officers. The Ernakulam district is divided into ten circles, each with ten labour officers. Calicut is divided into seven circles, each of which is headed by a labour officer.

In the fourth stage the researcher has selected two circles from each district based on the highest population rate of salespersons. Furthermore, the researcher randomly collected samples from each circle based on the proportion of the population of the salespersons.

The total number of salespersons working in big retail textile shops is 34309. The sample size for the study was calculated using Yamane (1967) method. In this study, a sample of 398 responses has been taken for the analysis[1]. Even though there is no general agreement on the minimum required sample size for Structural Equation Modelling (SEM), the research indicates that the sample size required depends on the number of parameters, indicators, included in the analysis, and the multivariate Normality of the data.

According to Jackson (2001), based on the estimate with multivariate normal data, a sample size of 200 to 400 numbers is recommended for statistical analyses. To ensure a safe sample size with a higher confidence interval and reduced margin of error, a sample size of 398 numbers has been selected for the analysis on a safer sample size basis.

[1] Refer the annexure for the detailed sample size estimation

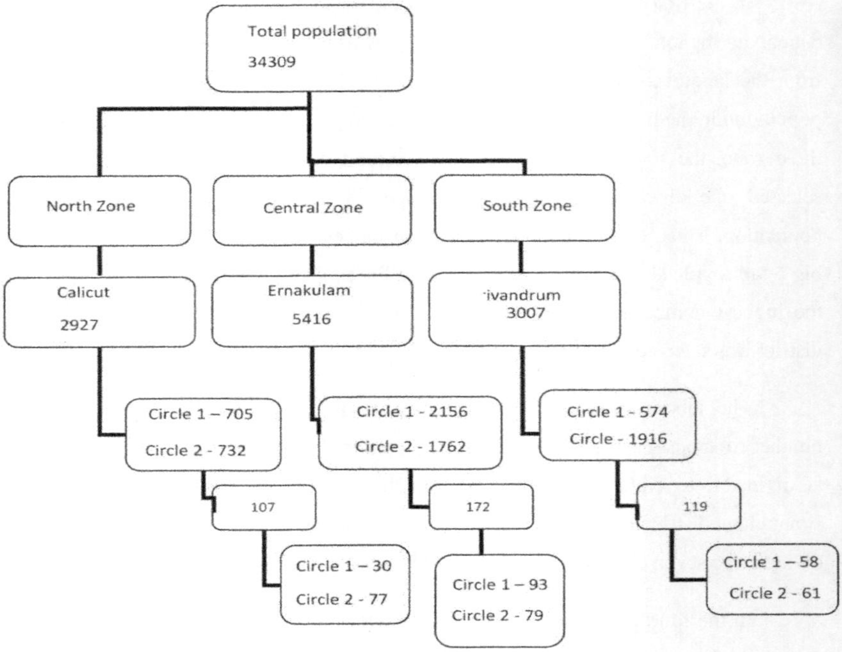

Figure1.3 Sampling Framework

1.13 Sources of Data

The study used primary data sources since it provided pertinent and current data on the subject of study. In addition, a structured interview schedule was used to obtain primary data from the salesperson.

The researcher has also considered various secondary data sources like related journals, statistical data of salespersons, data related to the total number of retail textile shops in Kerala, books and websites.

1.14 Measures

The data were collected through an interview schedule. The salespersons responded to all items on a five-point Likert scale from 1 (never) to 5 (always). Furthermore, it also consists of questions related to demographic characteristics of the salespersons like Age, Gender, Marital Status, Educational Qualification, Income, Experience, and Working Hours.

The survey instrument contains four sub-sections (Section A to Section D). Section A asked about the demographic characteristics of the salespersons. And study variables, like Psychosocial Work Environment (Section B), Job Burnout (Section C), and Turnover Intention (Section D), were measured.

1.14.1 Variables and Measurement Scales

The job Demand Resource Model is used to explain how demanding factors and resourceful factors in the work environment influence Job Burnout and Turnover Intention. Based on this theoretical model researcher has formulated variables and measurement scales. Following are the details of variables and scales that were used to collect data.

1.14.1.1 Psychosocial Work Environment

After the reliability test, all the scales except the psychosocial work environment showed good internal consistency. For improving the reliability of the psychosocial work environment out of thirteen variables, nine variables were adapted and eliminated variables are Role Conflict, Role Ambiguity, General Health, and Job Control. Seven variables were adopted from Copenhagen Questionnaire. This questionnaire was developed by Kristensen et al. (2005) at the National Centre for the Working Environment (NRCWE), Copenhagen, Denmark. It was developed as a tool for workplace assessment of the Psychosocial Work Environment. This study concerns the long version of COPSOQ I: Quantitative Demand (four items, e.g., "Do you have the feeling that your hours of work are long"?). Emotional Demand (three items, e.g., "Did your work put you in emotionally disturbing situations"?), Social support from Co-workers (three items, e.g., "Do you get any support and help from your co-workers"), Lack of Social Support from Supervisors (three items, e.g. "How often does your nearest superior talk with you about how nicely you carry out your job"?), Job

Insecurity (three items, e.g., "Do you have any difficulty to find another job if you become unemployed"?). Work-family Conflict (four items, e.g., "Personal relationships between you and family members").lack of Reward and Recognition(four items, e.g., "Are you getting a fair reward for the effort you put into the work"?), Abusive Supervision was assessed by Tepper, (2000), including five items (e.g., "My Supervisor scolds me in front of others"). The customer Incivility Scale established by Wilson and Holmvall (2013) was used to measure Customer Incivility. The sample item is "Does your customer always complain despite your efforts to assist them".

1.14.1.2 Job Burnout

Burnout Measure (Pines and Aronson1988) is a 21-item 5 points Likert scale designed to observe the level of Burnout among salespersons. Likert scale from never= zero to always = five on which salespersons are rating each of the three subscales, i.e. Emotional Exhaustion (seven items, e.g., "Feeling worthless"), Mental Exhaustion (seven items, e.g., "being unhappy"), and Physical Exhaustion (seven items, e.g.," Being tired").

1.14.1.3 Turnover Intention

The turnover intention scale (TIS-6) is a six-item scale by Bothma, C.F.C., & Roodt, G. (2013). The turnover intention was measured with 5-point Likert-type questions. A sample item is "how often have you considered leaving your job".

1.15 Pilot Study of the Questionnaire

A pilot study was carried out to test the questionnaire and gain knowledge about the relationship between the study variables. Before conducting the final study through the interview schedule method, 50 samples were collected from salespersons working in big retail textile shops under territorial jurisdiction Ernakulam district circle one. After the pilot study, a reliability test was conducted (Cronbach's alpha). All the scales except Psychosocial Work Environment have shown alpha values above 0.7. Nine of the thirteen Psychosocial Work Environment scales depicted a good internal consistency (α.70). For improving the reliability of the scale (Psychosocial Work Environment), out of thirteen variables, four variables were eliminated, and the eliminated variables are Role Conflict, Role Ambiguity, Job Control, and General Health.

1.16 Data Analysis Tools

The appropriate statistical tools and techniques were used to determine the study's final result. First, the researcher analysed the data gathered from salespersons using appropriate statistical techniques and tools, including exploratory factor analysis, confirmatory factor analysis, frequency distribution, and structural equation modeling (SEM).

1.17 Glossary of the Key Terms of the Study

1.17.1 Retail Textile Shops

Textile retailing sells textile products or merchandise, typically for personal or household use, either from a fixed location or through the association of subordinated services. Textile retailers are typically defined as organisations that purchase large quantities of textile products directly from manufacturers or importers or through a wholesaler and then sell individual product items or small quantities to the general public in shops or stores.

1.17.2 Salespersons

A retail salesperson is an employee of a retailer who is responsible for selling goods and services to the end-user in retail stores. He or she assists customers in locating items in a store or other retail establishment and persuades them to make purchases by explaining the benefits of the merchandise (Bureau of labor statistics,2020).

1.17.3 Psychosocial Work Environment

According to Warren (2001), a psychosocial work environment is defined as "non-physical aspects of the environment that have a psychological or physiological impact on the workers".

1.17.4 Quantitative Demand

Quantitative job demands are "those aspects of the work environment concerned with the amount and speed of work. That necessitates physical or psychological effort on the part of the employee" (van Emmerik & Peeters, 2009).

1.17.5 Emotional Demand

Employees who work in emotionally demanding jobs will experience emotionally charged interactions due to the nature of their jobs (Heuven et al., 2006).

1.17.6 Social Support from a Co-worker

Co-worker support is defined as "the extent to which one's co-workers are helpful, can be relied upon in times of need, and are receptive to work-related problems" (Menguc & Boichuk, 2012).

1.17.7 Lack of Social Support from Supervisor

Lack of Social support from supervisors is demonstrated in the form of no genuine concern for the needs of their subordinates (Iverson, 1996).

1.17.8 Abusive Supervision

It is referred to as "Abusive Supervision when it comes to how subordinates perceive the extent to which their supervisors participate in the sustained display of hostile verbal and nonverbal behaviours without physical contact" (Tepper,2000).

1.17.9 Lack of Reward and Recognition

Lack of Reward and Recognition in the workplace refers to the "Lack of acknowledging employees' efforts and their accomplishments through praise, respect and providing new opportunities for learning and advancement" (Mosley,2016).

1.17.10 Job insecurity

"Job insecurity reflects worries about the continuity of one's future employment or the threat of losing one's current job" (Sverke, Hellgren, & Näswall, 2002)

1.17.11 Work-family Conflict

"Work-family conflict is known as a specific type of inter-role conflict that arises when incompatible demands between work and family responsibilities" (Greenhaus & Beutell,1985).

1.17.12 Customer Incivility

"Salesperson's perception that the customer is treating them in an uncivil manner such as rudeness, disrespect and insults" (Pearson &Porath,2004).

1.17.13 Job Burnout

Pines & Aronson (1988) define Job Burnout as "a state of physical, emotional and mental exhaustion caused by long-term involvement in situations that are emotionally demanding."

1.17.14 Emotional Exhaustion

Emotional exhaustion, the second component of Job Burnout, involves "primarily feelings of helplessness, hopelessness, and entrapment" (Pines & Aronson 1988).

1.17.15 Mental Exhaustion

Mental exhaustion is the third component, characterised by "the development of negative attitude towards one's self, work and life itself"(Pines & Aronson 1988).

1.17.16 Physical Exhaustion

Physical exhaustion is characterised by "low energy, chronic fatigue, and weakness". (Pines & Aronson 1988).

1.16.17Turnover Intention

"The conscious and purposeful desire of an employee to leave his or her current organisation" (Tett &Meyer, 1993). While salesperson turnover can negatively affect a business, a steady sales team is critical to acquiring and engaging. On the other hand, a high turnover of salespeople results in significant recruitment and training expenditures (Sunder et al., 2017).

1.17 Period of Data Collection

The data collection period was from October 2019 to March 2020 in Kerala.

1.18 Scope of the Study

The current study is restricted to salespersons from big retail textile shops. The Psychosocial Work Environment has various social, psychological, and economic outcomes. However, the researcher focuses only on the effects of the Psychosocial Working Environment and its psychological outcomes such as Job Burnout and Turnover Intention.

According to the Shops and Commercial Establishment Act in section 2(S), shops or commercial establishments are classified into small, medium, and big categories. Small shops have no employees or up to five employees, medium shops have six or more but fewer than 20 employees, and large shops have 20 or more employees (Act, 2000).

According to recent research, when a shop's size expands, concern about psychological dangers also rises. In over 90 per cent of large business establishments, workplace stress is severe. Workplace violence or threats of violence are higher for larger venues than smaller establishments, and harassment follows the same pattern. Employees have unique psychological requirements. Supervisors are often ignorant of the full depth of these needs while supervising a large group of employees. However, it is relatively managed well in small and medium businesses.

Establishment size is a crucial variable when looking at the execution of preventative measures or processes connected to psychosocial risks. In terms of interventions, larger companies differ from smaller ones. There are differences between small and large businesses regarding job content and workplace transformation. When it comes to antisocial behaviour, larger workplaces have a higher per cent of employees reporting the problem than smaller ones.

Thus, this study focuses on the salespersons working in big textile shops to understand how these big textile shops manage the Psychosocial Work Environment of a large group of salespersons and whether there are any Job Burnout Issues and Turnover Intentions among salespersons. In Kerala, hundreds of salespersons work in major textile retailers like Seematti, Jayalakshmi, Kalyan Silks, Kalyan Sarees, Pothys, Swayamvara, Seeemas etc.

1.19 Limitations of the Study

This study is cross-sectional. The researcher has collected data from the salespersons only once, and the result may vary in a longitudinal study. The second limitation is that the findings cannot be generalised to the entire retail segment in Kerala. Samples were collected only from salespersons working in big retail textile shops. Third, this study has not investigated the relationship between the Psychosocial Work Environment and the personality traits of the salespersons. Based on the literature review, the researcher has assumed that if employees have a healthy work environment irrespective of their personality, they can maintain their well-being at the workplace (Burke &Deszea,2016; Golembiewski & Scicchitano, 1983; Maslach & Jackson, 1984).

1.20 Structure of the Chapters

The research work has been structured into five chapters to expand insights into the above points. A detailed sketch of each of them is given below.

Chapter 1: Introduction

Background of the Study, An Overview of the Retail Sector, Retail Textile Sector in India, Kerala Scenario in Textile Retailing, Salespersons in the Retail Textile Shops, Research Gap Identified, Significance of the Study, Problem Statements, Research Questions, Objectives of the Study, Hypotheses of the Study, Scope of the Study, Research Methodology, Glossary of the Key Terms of the Study, Limitations of the Study, Structure of the Study

Chapter 2: Review of Literature

This chapter deals with the Review of Literature in the arena of Psychosocial Work Environment, Job Burnout and Turnover Intention with a Research Gap

Chapter 3: Conceptual Framework of the Study

Chapter three elaborates the Conceptual Framework upon which the hypotheses are built.

Chapter 4: Data Analysis and Discussion

The statistical analysis results of the Data Collected are presented in this chapter. The Data Analysis was done systematically. Tables of Frequency and Percentage Analysis and Descriptive Statistics are used to present the findings. Confirmatory Factor Analysis with SEM, Reliability and Validity Analysis, Structural Equation Modelling of Hypotheses Testing, and Mediation Analysis.

Chapter 5: Findings, Suggestions, Implications, and Conclusion

Chapter five includes a Summary of Findings, suggestions, and Theoretical and Practical Implications. It also discusses the Scope for Further research in this area leading to the conclusion of this research.

1.21 Chapter Summary

This chapter introduces the background of the concepts and issues related to the Psychosocial Work Environment. Then, the research questions and significance of the study in light of Psychosocial Work Environment, Job Burnout, and Turnover Intention are presented. Next, the research objective was framed based on the research questions. Finally, the scope of the study, a detailed research methodology, glossary of the key terms of the study, limitations of the study are depicted. The next chapter deals with an extensive review of the literature.

CHAPTER 2

REVIEW OF LITERATURE

Researchers gain insights and focus on the study through conducting a review of the literature. The primary objective of this chapter is to summarise appropriate and related literature that serves as a base for this research and contextualise the current study within the existing body of knowledge. First, this chapter explains the comprehensive review of the Psychosocial Work Environment, its dimensions, and associated consequences like Job Burnout and Turnover Intention. The second section discussed related reviews of Psychosocial Work Environment, Turnover Intention, and Job Burnout research in the service sector. The concluding section of this chapter discusses the research gap identified through the literature review, which results in the formulation of the conceptual framework.

2.1 Psychosocial Work Environment

It was widely accepted that economic growth, improved production, and social steadiness depend on the various modes of working and living conditions and worker health and well-being. This realisation resulted in developing a comprehensive preventive strategy that considers physical and chemical hazards and the numerous psychosocial factors inherent in businesses, which can significantly impact workers' physical and mental well-being. Several decades of research have helped identify psychosocial work characteristics that are hazardous to employee health and well-being.

Psychosocial employment aspects (effort-reward imbalance, decision latitude, psychological pressures, and social support) and mental well-being among caregivers were studied by Bourbonnais et al. (2006). The study used a quasi-experimental design. The experimental group had fewer negative psychosocial factors one year after the intervention, but the control group had none. Supervisors' decision latitude and social support decreased significantly in both experimental and control groups. Sleeping issues and job-related burnout decreased significantly, although client-related and personal burnout increased. A considerable difference in all the psychological characteristics excluding decision latitude was seen after controlling for pre-intervention assessments. Other factors improved in the experimental group. Determining whether or not to keep engaging participants in the hospital will help reduce negative psychosocial aspects at work. The intensity of the intervention is predicted to be connected to its beneficial effects. However, long-standing consequences will be contingent on the organisation and employee commitment to own the procedure of recognising and reducing hostile psychosocial work conditions.

Reiner et al. (2007) led a longitudinal study to understand the association between sickness absence and the Psychosocial Work Environment. The study was adjusted for various factors, including participants who are exposed to violence and threats and participants who had high emotional demands, low influence at their work, poor management quality, and a higher number of sickness absences. Adjusting for sickness absence had a negligible influence on the majority of effect estimates. However, sickness absence days increased by 71 per cent whenever employees received a negative quartile rating on the psychosocial work environment. By improving the Psychosocial Work Environment and removing exposure to violence and threats, the study population's sickness absence would have been decreased by 32 per cent. This study discovered that exposure to violence was a significant predictor of absence. This study demonstrates that psychosocial work environments and exposure to violence contribute to sickness absence among service professionals. Avoiding negative consequences of psychosocial work environments benefits both company and employee.

Bonde (2008) conducted a follow-up study to examine the risk of psychosocial stresses and its major depressive symptoms in the workplace and assess the reason for the causation and job-related psychosocial factor. The study's quality was assessed using 22 factors. Population-based studies were identified, encompassing approximately 63 000 employees. In most investigations, validated multi-item measures were employed to assess perceived psychosocial stressors. Seven studies used clinical criteria to identify major depression, while another seven used symptom measures. The follow-up duration was between one and thirteen years. The prevalence of depressive illness varied considerably. The majority of studies shared relative weaknesses, including a lack of independent exposure and outcome measures and the possibility of confounding. This research demonstrates that exposure to poor psychosocial factors at the workplace is related to a high risk of subsequent depression or severe depressive symptoms.

Joling et al. (2008) conducted another study to determine whether work devotion and job resources are allied with work-related musculoskeletal illnesses over time and whether job resources mitigate the impact of work demand. The authors analyzed data from longitudinal three-stage research on workplace health amongst representative workers in the Netherlands. The initial poll of 3,100 associates of an established panel in 2004 was conducted via e-mail. The analysis included 1522 subjects with complete longitudinal data. This study demonstrates that job resources are critical for job commitment and for mitigating the harmful effect of high job demands.

A significant article by Pejtersen and Kristensen appears in the Scandinavian Journal of Work, Environment, and Health (2009). The authors investigated the Psychosocial Work Environment differences between 1997 and 2005 using national representative survey data from the Danish working class aged 20-60. Both samples were administered the Copenhagen Psychosocial Questionnaire, which allowed for a comprehensive assessment of psychosocial work conditions. Although approximately half of the psychosocial dimensions examined did not differ significantly between the two periods, the authors discovered that the 2005 sample reported a faster work pace than the 1997 sample. In addition, role conflict, workplace conflict, violent threats, and gossiping were more prevalent in 2005 than in 1997.

Additionally, employees' opportunities for influence and job control, career development opportunities, job meaning, and sense of community were lower in 2005 than in 1997. Additionally, the study indicated that colleagues' role clarity and social support have deteriorated over these years. Finally, a prominent feature of the study is that only two variables - supervisory social support and leadership quality - have improved over time.

Another study examines the psychological work environment disparities in 31 European countries. The survey included eighteen psychosocial variables. Poor decision-making freedom, job strain, sexual harassment, physical violence, mistreatment, discrimination, work-family issues, long work hours, high effort, job insecurity, compensation, low promotion and effort imbalance. Substantial variances in Psychosocial Work Environments were discovered between these nations. Additionally, they discovered a significant gender difference in psychological work characteristics. Women face significant difficulties due to a lack of discretionary skills, decision-making authority, workplace aggression, and a lack of job development. Men were concerned, however, about high psychological expectations, long work hours, a lack of support, a high effort-reward mismatch, and a work-family conflict (Niedhammer et al., 2012)

To emphasise the relevance of a positive Psychosocial Work Environment and improve the interaction between employees and the organisation, Beheshtifar (2012) conducted a study. According to the author's analysis, job satisfaction, increased burden, boring work, social support, and job control are the primary aspects influencing the Psychosocial Work Environment. They also discussed the negative and positive aspects of working in a psychological workplace. For example, suppose the Psychosocial Work Environment in the workplace is not conducive to employee happiness. In that case, it can lead to depression, stress, and anxiety, whereas a pleasant work environment can boost staff productivity and profits. As a result, organisations must pay more attention to promoting employee health and well-being.

Aminian, Moradi, and Eftekhari (2018) conducted a study on the Psychosocial Working Environment of office and operational employees in Iran's electricity distribution industry. Their working circumstances varied. Employees in operations are exposed to greater electromagnetic radiation, cold, heat, and sunlight, while office workers face quantitative and emotional demands.

2.1.1 Psychosocial Work Environment in the Retail Sector

Violante et al., (2005) led a cross-sectional survey of 3,702 employees from small and medium-sized supermarkets and hypermarkets in Italy to determine the prevalence of possible biomechanical, low back pain and psychosocial hazards. The various departments' data were gathered by a medical checklist, physical examination, and questionnaire, all completed by a certified medical doctor and analysed using complete biomechanical risk analysis. Findings show that (with an 82 per cent response rate), the 12-month prevalence of low back pain was 34.5 per cent (36.6 per cent for females and 30.7 per cent for men), with minor variations across supermarkets and hypermarkets. Furthermore, different types of low back pain were associated with severe psychosomatic symptoms associated with stress but not with job satisfaction.

A study was conducted among Danish retail workers about psychosocial and physical work environment characteristics and risk of low back pain. They investigated short-term changes in low back pain, and the influence of rest days and hectic workdays throughout a work week.low back pain, and long-term associations between occupational exposure assessed over a year. Participants were asked to rate their low back discomfort, physiological weariness, and perceived mental stress on a scale of 0–10. Questionnaires were used to track long-term pain development. In this study, physical and Psychosocial Work Environment characteristics were linked to acute and chronic low back pain. The collected data may be used to suggest changes to the work week to reduce the risk of low back pain among retail workers, as well as a fair daily lifting threshold. (Bláfoss et al., 2019).

Kalinien et al., 2021, examine the level of burnout among retail employees and its relationship to the Psychosocial Work Environment. The epidemiology study included 254 respondents from one Lithuanian retail network, with all respondents being female. Two measures were employed to evaluate their occupational stress and burnout: the HSE indicator tool and the Copenhagen burnout inventory (CBI). The study revealed an increased level of burnout—specifically, the frequency of client-related, personal, and work-related burnout. Spearman's correlation analysis found that all burnout subscales were substantially associated with job demands, control manager support, colleague support, and connections. Work demands and management support were found to be important predictors of burnout aspects in the multivariate logistic regression model. To summarise, in order to prevent occupational burnout among retail employees, it would be beneficial for occupational involvements to prioritise workload lessening and optimisation, and human resource management strategies should prioritise maintaining this.

2.1.2 Psychosocial Work Environment in India

The Indian workplace is increasingly evolving in response to the country's economic circumstances, technological advancements, corporate employment policies, and demographic trends. A change in universal economic development resulted in a slew of potentially serious issues, including environmental and occupational hazards, compensation problems, workplace safety, and psychosocial stress (Saiyed & Tiwari, 2004).

Pal and Saksvik (2008) undertook a study on the relationships between work-family conflict (WFC), job expectations, job control, social support, work-hour flexibility, family-work conflict (FWC) and workplace stress.27doctors and 328 nurses from Norway were included in the sample, as were 136 nurses and 111 doctors from India. The findings reveal that occupational stress predictors differ in India and Norway and between doctors and nurses. None of the research factors was an important predictor of job-related stress among Norwegian physicians. For Norwegian nurses, WFC, job expectations and a lack of workplace flexibility were significant occupational stress indicators. For Indian doctors, a lack of job control was a predictor of job stress, while for Indian nurses, a high family-work conflict and a lack of social support remained predictors of job stress.

Mehta and Parijat (2012) examined the effects of prevalent psychosocial factors on perceived musculoskeletal disorder outcomes among Indian information technology professionals. The data indicate that more than a quarter of respondents stated having existing shoulder/neck and low back pain. Additionally, two-thirds of respondents indicated that they had never received ergonomics awareness training. The most significant predictors of psychosocial risk variables for pain or discomfort and psychological stress were found to be co-worker support and psychological work demands. The result of this study emphasises the importance of specific psychological characteristics prevalent in the Indian information technology industry. As a result, intervention measures to address these risk factors are needed to reduce the risk of work-related musculoskeletal pain.

In response to an increase in the number of health complaints among call centre employees in an organisation, Nafeesa et al. (2018) conducted a study in Chennai, India, to survey the link between work-related musculoskeletal problems and psychological stress in the workplace. After gaining informed consent, data were collected using a questionnaire issued to the organisation's 155 call centre employees. According to the workers' perceptions, 65.8 per cent of participants experience an average degree of mental stress at work. Among the different psychological stressors at work, events outside one's control had the greatest impact on the majority of individuals (84.5 per cent). The neck area was the most frequent physical pain/discomfort experienced by research participants in the preceding 12-month period (53.5 per cent). The statistical study revealed a substantial correlation between musculoskeletal ailment prevalence and occupational mental stress. Additionally, this study concluded that a systematic strategy for risk reduction is necessary, including organisational, psychosocial, and physical work aspects.

2.1.3 Studies Related to Salespersons in the Retail Textile Shops

It was revealed in a case study by Usha P.E., titled "Determinants and Consequences of Women's Work in the Unorganized Sector," that women's work in textile shops in Trivandrum Corporation Area has negative consequences and determinants. Women in textile shops in Trivandrum are not provided with adequate space for eating and rest. Women working in this field do not receive a nominal wage increase based on the whims and fancies of the employer. Provident funds and insurance are only available to a small per cent of the workforce (two per cent).

It was determined that female salespersons in textile shops were satisfied with their jobs. This revealed that the majority of women were satisfied with the workplace amenities provided by their employers, such as a special refreshment room for female employees and a lodging or hostel facility, but that they did not have time to relax due to the long working hours without a break and the seasonal workload (Adeela,2014).

There are some key conclusions in this study about the socio-economic challenges of female workers in textile retail. A lack of basic sanitation, social security, and tight work schedules are among the issues cited in this report (Parvathy, 2018).

In informal textile retail shop in Chennai, women salespeople face numerous challenges as they balance work and family life. Most of these women are illiterate, unemployed, and poor. Workers' educational status is average secondary schooling. Almost 60 per cent of female workers are from marginalised groups. The study found that the sample respondents' social and economic status is poor, and they work in deprived and vulnerable conditions. The primary data show that women workers face many occupational health issues only after starting work. Women workers are also sexually and physically abused (K, S.,2019).

2.1.4 Research Gap Identified in the Literature of Psychosocial Work Environment

In a general context the psychosocial risks are rapidly becoming recognised as serious health concerns in developed or industrialised countries (Leka & Cox, 2008). Although these risks are concentrated in the industrialised world, they are becoming more widespread to developing nations due to changes in the nature of work.

However, in comparison to western countries, academic literature on psychosocial risk factors in the workplace in India is not as much, and little substantive data is available on nature, prevalence, antecedents and consequences, and extent of psychosocial risk factors in India. Therefore, this review shows that it has been a neglected study area to understand the effect of Psychosocial Work Environment on Job Burnout and Turnover Intention among salespersons in retail textile shops.

Additionally, following the literature assessment, the researcher added abusive supervision as a new variable for measuring the effect of the Psychosocial Work Environment of salespersons in retail textile shops, which was not included in the Copenhagen Psychosocial Work Environment questionnaire.

Most prior studies on salespersons in retail textile shops have focused on women. So, the researcher included both male and female salespersons in this study to have a better understanding of both gender's viewpoints

2.2 Psychosocial Work Environment and Job Burnout

Susann and colleagues (2012) conducted a study with the goal of determining the prevalence of burnout among female and male police officers in Sweden, as well as its relationship to the physical strain, psychosocial work environment, and stress of conscience. When compared to other studies, such as those conducted on police officers in Norway and the Netherlands, the prevalence of emotional exhaustion and depersonalisation was higher. Women's emotional exhaustion was found to be significantly associated with the high demand, stress of conscience, and the organisational climate. It was the stress of conscience, decision, and high demand that caused men to lose their emotions. In our model of depersonalisation, only stress of conscience and gender were statistically significant contributors to the process of depersonalisation. Further research is required in order to develop interventions among Swedish police officers aimed at reducing levels of burnout.

Personal burnout in employees who work with people who have intellectual disabilities is investigated by Agnessa (2013), as is the relationship between personal burnout and health and work-related outcomes in employees who work with people who have intellectual disabilities. On the basis of this research, a cross-sectional survey in northern Germany and 30 residential facilities was carried out (N = 409; response rate: 45%). The standard version of the Copenhagen Psychosocial Questionnaire in German was used in this study. Multiple logistic regression analysis revealed that characteristics such as work–privacy conflict, emotional demands, role conflicts, job uncertainty, and feedback were predictors of personal burnout in the workplace. The current study demonstrates that refining the psychosocial work environment at the organisational level can help mitigate personal burnout as well as other negative consequences such as dissatisfaction and the intention to leave one's current position.

Cheng et al. (2013) conducted a survey to determine the relationship between self-rated health (SRH) and burnout in psychosocial workplace atmosphere. A valid technique was used to measure workplace-related aspects such as workplace justice, job demands, employment insecurity, working hours, and job control. A single item scale was employed to assess health-related variables, including self-rated health measures, the CBI (Copenhagen Burnout Inventory), was utilised to assess burnout. The instruments were administered to a male (N=20,454) and female (N=16,875) sample. The findings indicated that a low degree of workplace justice contributed to high burnout and poor health condition.

The financial sector has been impacted by the changes that have occurred in the modern economy. Bank employees are frequently confronted with time constraints, high work demands, and job stress, all of which contribute to the development of burnout symptoms. Among bank employees, the goal of this study was to investigate the relationship between burnout symptoms and exposure to Psychosocial Work Environments. 10446 bank employees were polled in northern Brazil's states of Pará and Amapá. A self-administered questionnaire was used to assess sociodemographic variables, burnout, and two job stress models (Demand–Control–Support and Effort–Reward

Imbalance). Results were compared between the two models. Acute level of burnout (ALB) is characterised by symptoms that are mild to moderate in intensity, while severe level of burnout (SLB) is characterised by symptoms that are severe in intensity (HLB). Logistic regression was used to estimate the relationships between the two levels of burnout and the two stress models, while also controlling for relevant factors. According to the findings, psychosocial work environment in the financial sector, such as high strain, limited social support from workplace, high effort/low return, and excessive commitment, may be hazard factors for bank employees who experience moderate to severe levels of burnout symptoms (Maria et al., 2008).

Padyab (2016) examines the relationship between burnout and the psychosocial work environment, coping strategies, and moral stress, of patrolling police officers in Sweden. The majority of the variables, including psychological demand, social support, decision-making latitude and coping measures, were associated with burnout. To determine the predictive value a hierarchical multiple regression analysis was used. The findings of this study indicate that while examining the influence of the psychosocial work environment on burnout, it is necessary to take conscience stress and degrees of social support and choice latitude into account.

Khan et al. (2018) in their descriptive study hypothesise that an adaptive working environment can help to maintain good workplace health, which will help to prevent doctor burnout. This study demonstrates that burnout plays a mediating role between psychosocial work characteristics and depressive and anxiety symptoms. It is important, according to this study, to mitigate burnout through job autonomy and to reduce work-related pressure before it progresses to severe psychological morbidity and disability.

A study in various human service sector, a total of 824 individuals were selected for the three-year follow-up analysis. The study aim was to determine if burnout predicts sickness absence curses and sickness absence days among human professionals working in the field. The research was carried out in a number of different human service sector. It is suggested by the findings of the study that burnout may be a contributing factor to sick leave. Variations in burnout level over time were related with similar variations in sickness absence suggests that preventing burnout may be beneficial in terms of decreasing sickness absence in the long run (Borritz et al., 2019).

2.2.1 Job Burnout in the Retail Sector

People who work in marketing as boundary spanners, such as, sales representatives and customer service representatives are particularly vulnerable to burnout. Specifically, the authors describe burnout and hypothesis that burnout serves as a partial mediator between critical behavioural and psychological job outcomes and role pressures. According to the responses of 377 customer service workers, their levels of burnout are high when compared to other burnout-prone jobs, and burnout has consistent, significant, and dysfunctional effects on their behavioural and psychological outcomes, according to their responses. Furthermore, burnout mediates the negative effects of role stress on employment outcomes, whereas the positive effects of role stress are unmediated (Singh et al., 1994).

Johnson (2013) investigated the relationship between age, stress management skills and burnout in the context of customer stressors. From 273 retail workers, age is associated with client concerns but not directly with stress management measures. When confronted with unfavourable customers, cynicism is less among aged employees. Furthermore, aged employees' stress management practises of active coping and emotion control and were found to be associated with a reduction in both emotional exhaustion and cynicism. The results of the professional efficacy study were consistent with previous findings. The use of humour and denial had only minor effects on the effects of age. These findings were consistent in high-stress situations, with younger employees demonstrating less success in implementing these strategies to reduce levels of emotional tiredness and cynicism. In conclusion this article highlights the abilities of older workers while also disproving their perceived limitations.

Vignoli et al. (2021) Investigate the association of bad customer relationships employee fatigue and general wellness. The data were acquired anonymously via a self-report questionnaire administered at a large-scale retail corporation in Italy. The sample consisted of 610 employees (70 per cent of whom were female) employed in 28 supermarkets. Negative customer interactions were shown to be connected with increased levels of emotional dissonance, which was found to be associated with high level of burnout and, ultimately, with increased levels of poor general health. This study is helpful to understand how unfavourable customer relationships might initiate a health impairment process in employees, resulting in increased levels of burnout and poor overall health. Furthermore, the findings imply that organisations whose work activities include daily contact with consumers should undertake training activities to help employees improve their customer service abilities, such as how to control their emotions at work.

This study was to inspected burnout among retail network employees as well as the Psychosocial Work Environment in which they worked. A total of 254 female employees from a Lithuanian retail chain (n = 254) participated in the study. The work-related stress indicator tool and the Copenhagen Burnout Inventory, both developed by the HSE management standards, were used to assess their stress and burnout (CBI). Individual, work, and client-related burnout were all found to be prevalent. Occupational demands, control manager support, colleague support, and social connections were all found to be associated with burnout. With the help of multivariable logistic regression, we were able to determine the independent relationships between health and safety indicators and burnout subscales. The demands of the job and the assistance provided by the manager were significant contributors to all aspects of burnout. As a result, occupational treatments should emphasise workload reduction and optimization in order to reduce job burnout among retail employees, while human resource management should ensure that these efforts are sustained (Kaliniene et al,2021).

Burnout among salespersons is a major source of concern for sales organisations worldwide. Because of this, the authors of this article investigate whether specific coping methods, as described by Thoits (1982) in his Coping-Mediational Model, can reduce the negative impact of sales manager assistance on the burnout of salespersons. More specifically, this study investigates whether emotion-focused coping styles and problem-focused coping styles have a moderating effect on the sales manager assistance on experiences of emotional fatigue in a field sales environment. Sales managers who are supportive of their employees have a significant negative direct impact on their employees' emotional weariness, according to the findings of the study. The findings also support the notion that sales manager assistance encourages salespersons problem-solving coping mechanisms, which in turn helps them feel less emotionally exhausted. Sales manager assistance, had no significant effect on salesperson's use of emotion-focused coping;

however, emotion-focused coping is associated with significantly increased emotional tiredness (Lewin & Sager,2008).

2.2.2 Job Burnout Studies in the Indian Work Environment

The effects of burnout and work-related stress are well-documented in developed countries, but there is a paucity of research on the subject in India. Lack of personal accomplishment and Emotional Exhaustion are the two burnout dimensions in which secondary school teachers score moderately, but Depersonalization is a dimension where they score poorly (Shukla & Trivedi, 2008).

Another article investigates the effect of job burnout and how it leads to psychological outcomes like job dissatisfaction, lack of commitment, intention to quit and a behavioural outcome like poor job performance among customer service representatives in Indian call centres, and the results indicate that job burnout, has a substantial effect (Surana & Anup, 2009).

Job burnout significantly impacts organisational politics in Chennai's Banking Sector due to numerous independent variables such as job attitude and job involvement. The t-test was used to determine the primary cause of Job Burnout in an organisation. Specifically, the scope of this study is limited to a small number of public and new private sector banks in the Chennai metropolitan region. In Chennai, the researcher visited eight public sector banks and five non-public sector banks. Approximately one hundred and twenty surveys were distributed, with 60 coming from public sector banks and another 60 coming from new private sector banks. The findings revealed that bank employees in both the public and private sectors experienced periods of emotional exhaustion and burnout as a result of their jobs, and that they found it difficult to work cooperatively with others (Sowmya &Panchanatham, 2011).

The examination of interviews with young knowledge workers in India's information technology services sector showed that a lack of integration with the job and the organisation as a whole, underemployment, a stressful job and an exhausting work environment, anxiety and worry about talent replacement and downsizing all contributed to their Burnout (Packirisamy et al.,2017). Identifying predictors of police officer burnout confirmed the crucial role of organisational elements in police management and administration. Additionally, the data highlighted the critical role of a supportive climate in reducing burnout as a contextual protective factor (Anand.2017).

A thorough review and analysis found that healthcare professionals (HCPs) in India regularly experience burnout due to the growing workload and poor working conditions (Kesarwani, Husaain & George, 2020). Additionally, psychiatrists in India are prone to burnout (Sharma, 2018).

Dhusia et al. (2019) studied the occurrence of burnout among resident physicians and concluded that it is a reason for grave worry. In India, factors such as long work hours, inadequate facilities, and physical and mental abuse of physicians by patients and seniors contribute to a high rate of occupational burnout among medical practitioners. The sample included 300 resident physicians who worked in public sector institutions around Mumbai. Burnout was quantified on three levels: personal, work-related, and client-related. The high frequency of burnout syndrome among resident doctors in public sector hospitals is concerning, as it has a detrimental effect on the medical practitioners' physical and mental health and productivity and motivation. As a result, stress management measures should be promoted in hospitals in order to promote work-life balance.

2.2.3 Research Gap Identified

In the Indian retail work environment, there is a near absence of research on "burnout". Thus, it is relevant to understand job burnout of salespersons due to the psychosocial risk factors in the retail work environment. To understand the causes and consequences of job burnout in the retail textile sector is helpful to prevent the issues and retailers can perform well in the current business world.

2.3 Psychosocial Work Environment and Turnover Intention

Spain's emergency medical and nursing staff were studied by Escribà et al., (2006) to determine the relationship between the Psychosocial Work Environment and burnout among them. The second aim was to determine whether the Psychosocial Work Environment had a different impact on burnout in doctors and nurses, as opposed to other professionals. Because of this, a survey was led among 945 emergency physicians and nursing staff members in the country of Spain. According to the demand-control model developed by Karasek and Johnson, burnout was the outcome variable, and the Psychosocial Work Environment was the explanatory variable in the study. As a result, only doctors experienced a negative effect on the emotional exhaustion dimension when their control was low. Burnout syndrome, on the other hand, was found to be more prevalent among those who had little control over their work environment.

Clausen et al., (2010) investigated specifically affective organisational commitment, positive work-related states, and meaning at work. According to a cohort study conducted in Denmark, 730 employees of eldercare services were compared to 5,262 employees who are not changed occupations during the study's follow-up period. At the outset of the study, participants were asked about their positive job-related feelings and psychosocial work characteristics. Initially, variables related to psychosocial work predicted turnover. The mediators, on the other hand, had a negative effect on the relationships between psychological work factors and turnover. As a result, positive job-related feelings have an impact on the long-term relationship between psychosocial work characteristics and turnover. In addition, the findings suggest that improving positive work-related states as well as the psychosocial work environment can help to reduce employee turnover in the eldercare industry.

A longitudinal study conducted in China, by Li et al., (2010) discussed this concept in the context of a psychosocial work environment assessment using the Copenhagen Psychosocial Questionnaire, which was used to assess the psychosocial work environment (COPSOQ). There was a total of 3,088 registered female nurses who worked in hospitals who were eligible for the multivariate logistic regression baseline analyses; a total of 1,521 registered female nurses who worked in hospitals were eligible for the multivariate Poisson regression follow-up analyses; and a total of 3,088 registered female nurses who worked in hospitals were eligible for the multivariate logistic regression baseline analyses. It was found that a variety of psychosocial factors experienced at work – in particular, increased emotional demands at work, decreased job meaning at work, decreased commitment to the workplace, and decreased job satisfaction – were associated with turnover intention in both baseline and prospective analyses, even after controlling for a number of confounding variables. According to the findings, a negative psychosocial work environment is associated with a higher likelihood of having an intention to leave among Chinese registered nurses. Nursing workforce retention may be improved as a result of improvements to the psychosocial work environment on the other hand.

Another investigation by Li et al. (2013) looked into the predictive value of a broad range of psychosocial work factors in relation to the likelihood of a desire to leave the nursing profession. There were 7,990 female nurses in the study, who came from eight different countries: Italy, France, Belgium, Germany, China, Poland, and Slovakia. The survey used a structured questionnaire to gather information on job hardship, effort-reward imbalance, employment opportunities, and the intention to leave the nursing profession. Data were analysed using multilevel logistic regression to determine the relationships between variables. During the follow-up, it was discovered that poor promotion prospects and favourable job opportunities were both independently associated with a new desire to leave the nursing profession. Job stress, on the other hand, appeared to have less predictive power. The findings indicate that initiatives to improve the psychosocial work environment, particularly the reciprocity of effort and reward, may aid in the retention of nurses and the alleviation of the worldwide nursing shortage.

To determine and quantify which psychosocial work environment characteristics have the most significant impact on one-year employee turnover rates in a hospital context, Mathisen et al. (2021) conducted an observational cohort study in which they divided the participants into occupational groups. There were 24 385 public hospital employees who participated in the Danish Hospital Employees Well-Being cohort in 2014. The study population was made up of these individuals. The findings revealed that 2552 (10.5 per cent) of the 24 385 participants had quit their jobs during the one-year follow-up. As a result, improving the psychological work environment could have prevented up to 44 percent of this turnover, according to the authors' estimates. The satisfaction with job prospects, overall job contentment, and bullying were the areas where hypothetical improvements were the most significant. Nursing staff had a better chance of preventing turnover than physicians and other members of the healthcare team. As a result, improvements in the psychosocial work environment, particularly among nurses, have the potential to significantly reduce employee turnover.

2.3.1 Job Burnout and Turnover Intention

Jacob and Abraham, (1999) conducted research to examine the relationship between burnout dimensions and the intention of female teachers in Israel to leave their current positions. Burnout Scale items were factor analysed and classified into three categories: physical, emotional, and mental. Then, using multiple regression analysis, the items were correlated with the intention to leave by the authors of the Burnout Scale (A. Pines et al., 1981). Physical and mental exhaustion were found to have a positive and statistically significant impact on the intention to leave. The effect of emotional exhaustion was not significant, and neither were the ages of the teachers involved. Both burnout and the turnover intention were found to be inversely and significantly correlated with tenure.

Using the context of Arabic culture, Muhammad and Hamdy (2005) investigated the relationships that exist between individuals who have experienced burnout, supervisory support and work outcomes such as job satisfaction, organisational commitment, and a desire to leave their jobs. When it comes to the relationship between burnout experience and work results, supervisory support is considered to be a moderator. According to data collected from 308 Arab employees at seven Kuwaiti businesses, experienced burnout is negatively associated with job satisfaction, and both organisational commitment and burnout are positively associated with intention to leave. However, supervisory support moderates the relationship between experienced burnout and work outcomes, according to the researchers.

Based on their findings, emotional exhaustion, depersonalization, and a diminished sense of personal accomplishment are all associated with increased turnover intentions, according to Choi et al., (2012). As a result of emotional exhaustion, there was a significant increase in depersonalization. Based on the findings of the moderating variables, it can be concluded that not all therapies are beneficial for all three components of job burnout. The authors conducted a survey of 287 customer service representatives from seven call centres as part of their investigation. In order to mitigate the negative impact of depersonalisation on turnover intentions, extensive attention was paid to supervisors' assistance and support. Under conditions of depersonalisation, monetary rewards were found to decrease turnover intentions, whereas they were found to increase turnover intentions under conditions of diminished personal achievement. Choosing career paths that allow for less depersonalization and more personal accomplishment can help to reduce turnover intentions.

Rajendran et al., (2020) decided to use the job demands-resources (JD-R) model to determine the correlates of teacher turnover intent among male and female teachers at the primary 580 and secondary 675 levels. Multigroup structural equation modelling revealed that workplace demands (such as workload and student misbehaviour), as well as the personal demand for work–family harmony, were all positively associated with emotional exhaustion, which is the central characteristic of burnout, according to the findings. All demands are connected to the goal of turnover in a secondary way, through emotional exhaustion. Neither emotional exhaustion nor turnover intention were found to differ significantly between the teacher groups, and only a moderate amount of stress was reported as a result of student misbehaviour. Work–family conflict was found to be the most significant predictor of emotional exhaustion in both male and female teachers. Results indicate that personal demands should be considered alongside professional demands when analysing job-related outcomes among Australian teachers, and that the JD-R is a good theory for understanding job-related outcomes among Australian teachers

Burnout, which has become a modern epidemic, is the most common reason for educators to leave their jobs in the United States. Following the guidelines of the job demands-resources theory, this study investigates the underlying mechanisms of burnout and the direct relationships between job characteristics such as job demands and job resources, with turnover intention, as well as work engagement among a sample of educators in the United States. According to the findings, burnout acted as a moderator in the relationship between job demands and work engagement, as well as in the relationship between job resources and turnover, among other things. Main findings of the study emphasise the importance of elucidating the causes and consequences of burnout, as well as the contribution to the field of burnout research by looking at underlying components of burnout such as work demand and the intention to leave (Russell et al., 2020).

The fact that China has made significant strides in modernising its primary healthcare system does not diminish the fact that high turnover intention remains a significant social problem. Job burnout and job satisfaction have a significant impact on the intention to leave a job. Among primary healthcare workers in central China, the purpose of this cross-sectional study was to gain insight into job burnout, job satisfaction, and the intention to leave their positions. Maximum likelihood estimation was used to investigate the relationship between job satisfaction and job burnout and intention to quit. According to the findings, there is a positive relationship between job burnout and the intention to quit. Other potential determinants of turnover intentions, such as job stress, social support from one's work environment, and mental health were not taken into consideration in this study. (Ran et al., 2020).

2.3.2 The Turnover Intention in the Indian Service Industry

Dasgupta (2015) conducted a study in which he developed an integrated model of nurses' intentions to leave the profession. The findings indicate that a lack of adequate organisational and supervisory support, an unpleasant work environment, and a low level of core self-evaluation all have a significant impact on the intention of qualified and experienced nurses in India to leave their positions in their respective organisations.

A study by Verma and Chaurasia (2016) was carried out in order to create a productive and healthy work environment for employees and to motivate these employees to take an active role in the organisation by providing them with a sense of satisfaction and involvement. As a result, the most significant factor influencing turnover intention is a lack of positive appraisal from upper management. In addition, equitable compensation is a critical factor in determining whether or not to leave a company. Following that, factors such as job security, teamwork, training programmes, fringe and welfare benefits, and work stress are taken into consideration.

In India's small and medium-sized information technology companies, annual turnover rates are now in the range of 25-30 percent (Tejaswi 2010), with some mid-sized companies experiencing turnover rates of up to 40 percent among their project managers (Sengupta and Mishra 2010). In the Indian information technology sector, job stress has a significant positive correlation with employee turnover intentions, growth & development, culture & process, training, and compensation benefits, and all significantly impact employee turnover intentions (K & Rao, 2019).

Employees in the business process outsourcing industry in India's lower and middle levels of enterprises demonstrated inconsistent results when asked about their intention to leave their jobs.Gender and marital status were found to have no statistically significant relationship with the intention to turn over a business. Age, monthly income, and shifts, on the other hand, all confirmed that there is a statistically significant relationship between turnover intention and turnover intention among business process outsourcing professionals. Younger BPO employees in entry-level positions demonstrated a greater proclivity to resign than their more experienced counterparts. Similarly, employees from lower-income groups were less likely to remain with their existing employers. The survey discovered that employees who worked afternoon and night hours were more likely to leave their current companies than employees who worked morning shifts (Afroz & Haque,2020).

2.3.3 Turnover Intention in Indian Retail Sector

According to The Retail Workforce Study (2014), the retail sector has a high labour absorption rate compared to other industries and a high employee turnover rate.

Eight significant factors affecting employees' intention to quit in India's organised retail sector were identified in a study. This included management practises compensation and benefits, career development, training and development, social support, working conditions, communication systems, and security measures (Priyanka & Dubey, 2016). Another study identified eight critical factors that influence employees' intent to quit. This included management practises compensation and benefits, career development, training and development, social support, working conditions, communication systems, and security measures (Dubey,2017). Another study discovered that work-related stress, organisational commitment, realistic job information, work environment, and job satisfaction all influence frontline employees' intention to quit. Additionally, it was discovered that job satisfaction and realistic job information significantly have positive effects (Pandey et al., 2019).

The study surveyed 347 salespeople from various retail firms in Delhi. The relationship between job satisfaction, core self-evaluation and turnover intentions. Additionally, the study sought to determine whether core self-evaluation acts as a moderator of the association between turnover intention and job satisfaction. Multiple regression analysis revealed that both job satisfaction and core self- evaluation were inversely associated with turnover intentions. Additionally, it was discovered that core self-evaluation moderated the association between job satisfaction and turnover intentions, resulting in a stronger relationship for employees with poor core self-evaluation. The study suggests that managers should implement initiatives to boost job satisfaction in order to mitigate the sector's high attrition rate. Personality traits play a moderating influence in the relationship between job satisfaction and turnover intentions, which they must be aware of. (Grau & Heuschmann,2020).

2.3.4 Research Gap Identified in the Literature of Turnover Intention

Researchers have discovered a wide range of factors that contribute to the rising problem of turnover intention such as poor working condition lack of social support, high emotional demand may result in psychologically detached managers in the public sector (Yuanjie & Zhong,2021). Another study report depicts that psychosocial work environment of coaches such as social community at work, and trust regarding management are some of the positive elements to improve their psychosocial work environment. Coaches' emotional demands were associated with low mental-health scores and higher levels of behavioral-stress symptoms and burnout (Hinojosa et.al). Another study analyzed whether unfavorable psychosocial work environment could predict nurses' intention to leave in China. The findings show that increased emotional demand, decreased meaning of work and decreased job satisfaction were associated with turnover intention among nurses.

In India no empirical studies on the effect of psychosocial work environment on turnover intention and the mediating function of job burnout studies have been undertaken in the retail textile sector. India lags in implementing or identifying relevant interventions and effective regulations to reduce psychosocial risks at work as a developing country with the largest working-age population So, the researcher is expecting high prevalence of psychosocial risks among salespersons in the retail textile shops.

2.4 Chapter Summary

The chapter discussed the various literatures of Psychosocial Work Environment, Job Burnout and Turnover Intention. Further the relationship between these variables were discussed. The research gaps were identified based on each study variables. It provides insights on the status of the empirical research carried out in the area. The next chapter discusses the theoretical framework for the study in detail.

CHAPTER 3

CONCEPTUAL FRAMEWORK OF THE STUDY

Reviewing the extensive literature, the researcher observed that authors employed a wide range of antecedent variables and result variables in their empirical analyses. Therefore, the researcher concentrated on the core aspects of the proposed study based on the available and relevant reading to the subject matter. The following section of the chapter discusses the conceptual and specific theoretical backdrop, relevant variables selected, and its relationships, which serve as the basis for this study. The chapter ends with the conceptual framework.

3.1 Conceptual Focus of the Study

The core of this research is that long-term high job demand, which salespersons do not correctly recover, may lead to Job Burnout and low job resources activate Turnover Intention. The main antecedents of Job Burnout and Turnover Intentions include Quantitative Demand, Emotional Demand, Abusive Supervision, Lack of Supervisory Support, Lack of Support from co-workers, Lack of Reward and Recognition, Job Insecurity, Work-Family Conflict, and Customer Incivility.

Therefore based on the theoretical perspectives and the proposed hypotheses, the salesperson's work environment has prolonged high job demands such as Quantitative Demand, Emotional Demand, Abusive Supervision, and Job Insecurity. Moreover, low job resources like Lack of Reward and Recognition, Lack of Support from Supervisor or Co-worker, low Family Support, and high Customer Incivility leads to Turnover Intention, which has been considered one of the significant negative outcomes of Job Burnout. So, this study also tests the mediating effect of Job Burnout between Psychosocial Work Environment and Turnover Intention.

3.1.1 Psychosocial Work Environment

Psychosocial workplace conditions, frequently denoted as the Psychosocial Work Environment, have developed a consistent factor in occupational health research (Hammer et al.,2004). The Psychosocial Work Environment emerges from the interrelationship between the workplace and the individual.

Numerous research is available in this area, which explains how individuals interact with their workplace determined by working conditions and human capacities. Thus, the workplace setting is an interaction of many factors, including job demands, support from co-workers and administrators, physical conditions, social setting, executive practices and employment state.

Employees are the organisation's most valuable asset. Employees who are not satisfied with their work environment or lives will exhibit decreased productivity and less commitment to their jobs.

Studies have established a link between employee well-being and reduced workplace quitting, improved physical health and high employee performance (Wright & Cropanzano, 2000; Wright & Bonett, 1997; Richman et al., 2005). Lack of employee well-being can have a detrimental effect on both workers and employers.

When work conditions and personal factors are in balance, a profession fosters a sense of purpose and self-confidence, increases motivation and working ability, and improves health. On the other hand, an imbalance between individual needs, capabilities, potential, and environmental factors results in different outcomes.

Table 3.1

Definitions of Psychosocial Work Environment

Authors	Definitions
Eriksson (1997)	"Those variables that are influenced by the nature of the work, its organisation, and the social relationships in the workplace."
Oxford English Dictionary (2012)	"The effect of social factors on an individual's mind or behaviour, as well as the relationship between behavioural and social factors."
Lindstrom et al. (2000)	"The Psychosocial Work Environment as a compound system that includes the work, the workers, and the environment".
Warren (2001)	"Non-physical aspects of the work environment that have a psychological or physiological impact on the workers."

3.1.2 Historical Evolution of the Psychosocial Work Environment Concept

Although the sociotechnical system approach to improving job design and work organisation was born in England, most of the earliest interventions were conducted in Scandinavian nations such as Norway and Sweden from the mid-1960s onwards. As a result, the collaborative and participatory approach with workers was developed in Scandinavian nations. At the same time, the "Quality of Work-life" movement began to develop in the United States, where the earlier technological determinism of work conditions changed towards a more holistic approach to job design.

This research began to prosper in Scandinavian nations in the 1960-1970s when social science and health research were combined for the investigation and reforming of work life. Bertil Gardell and some other researchers were pioneers in this field. The study conducted by University of Michigan on job demands and workers' health, had a strong influence on the research approach and on the definition of a good or healthy work environment. In Finland, the Scandinavian influence began in the 1970s.

Especially at the end of the 1970s and the beginning of the 1980s, research and intervention to promote a good work environment proceeded along the same lines in Finland as in other northern and middle European countries. In the beginning, they strongly emphasised well-being criteria and recently also the mastery of work. The orientation towards health was partly due to the close relation to research on occupational health at the Finnish Institute of Occupational Health.

Especially at the end of the 1970s and the beginning of the 1980s, research and intervention to promote a good work environment proceeded along the same lines in Finland as in other northern and middle European countries

The quality of work-life criteria, which is to a great extent same as the main job stressors, has been applied to job redesign and organisational intervention. The measurement of job characteristics and their relation to health acts as a starting point for health promotion and organisational development, and it continues to influence these characteristics. In real-life situations at the workplace, contextual factors are important. In traditional empirical research, these contextual factors are often excluded. However, these factors have often proved to be the most central and most important prerequisites or hindrances to successful intervention.

In 1974, the World Health Assembly discussed the psychosocial factors that affect workers' health at work and their overall health. (Safety and Series, 1984.)

The first research publication in English-language with the title "Psychosocial Work Environment" was issued in 1982. It is entitled "Myocardial infarction risk and psychosocial work environment in the male Swedish workforce," and was authored by Swedish academicians Töres Theorell and Lars Alfredsson and the American researcher Robert Karasek.

Beginning in 1984, the World Health Assembly discussed the psychosocial factors that affect workers' health and its impact on their overall health. (Safety and Series, 1984.). As a result, the socio-psychological conditions people encounter in the workplace, considering the Psychosocial Work Environment, have developed a standard factor of occupational health studies (Hammer et al., 2004).

Furthermore, in the succeeding years, the phrase was primarily employed in papers written by Swedish and American authors. For example, in 1991, twenty-one scholars contributed to the book "The Psychosocial Work Environment: Work Organization, Democratization, and Health". The majority were from Sweden and the United States (Johnson & Johansson, 1991).

During the 1990s and 2000s, researchers in Psychosocial Work Environment began to incorporate new concepts, such as organisational justice, the balance between efforts and rewards, workplace bullying, and workplace social capital, which were previously unexplored (Siegrist,1996; Elovainio et al.2019; Kouvonen et al.2006; Einarsen & Skogstad, 1996). Psychosocial Work Environment research became more "psychological," in the sense that research became increasingly focused on whether or not workers feel treated fairly and respected, as well as the emotional effects of work tasks, procedures, or behaviours by colleagues, clients, supervisors, and customers, as well as the emotional effects of work tasks, procedures, or behaviours by clients and customers

In accordance with this idea, the 13th European Congress of Work and Organizational Psychology, held in Stockholm in 2007, emphasised the "win-win" nature of favourable working circumstances in its congress topic, "Sustainable Work: Promoting Human and Organisational Vitality."

This growth has been aided by the Scandinavian Journal of Work, Environment, and Health. Articles have been issued on various topics, including the possible impact of work circumstances on sickness absenteeism (Virtanen et al.2008; Josephson et al. 2008). Other research has shed light on gender differences in psychosocial aspects and examined how to create attractive work environments to increase job commitment and minimise the detrimental effect of workplace demands on musculoskeletal illnesses (Hooftman et al., 2009; Joling et al., 2008). Additionally, the journal has published narrative reviews and meta-analyses that have made significant contributions to the body of knowledge (Stansfeld & Candy, 2006; Akerstedt, 2006).

It is now widely recognised that excessive job demands, job insecurity, role conflict, time pressure, poor leadership, violence at work, and long work hours can negatively influence an employee's well-being and productivity. Control at work, participation in decision-making, relevant feedback, clear goals, social support, and skill utilisation, are the some of the important beneficial factors of good psychosocial work conditions (Gardner et al., 2002).

The Psychosocial Work Environment encompasses various aspects of work, including job demands, job control, effort and reward, excessive workloads, high emotional exhaustion, lack of autonomy, and position conflict (Beheshtifar, 2012). On the other hand, psychosocial factors reflect the interaction of social and psychological factors. This dynamic interaction is the core of psychosocial research. The Psychosocial Work Environment issues are widely regarded as one of the most pressing workplace challenges in todays and future societies.

Bullying, abusive supervision,and workplace violence are some examples of psychosocial risks. According to a large body of evidence, work-related psychosocial risks can have an adverse influence on mental, physical, and emotional well-being, as well as the performance of organisations and society. They are the result of ineffective job design, management, organisation, and social background. Resulting in negative psychological, physical, and social outcomes such as absenteeism, lack of motivation, job-related stress,and disturbed social interaction at the workplace.

These risk factors are strongly intertwined with the changing nature of work. Psychosocial risks are the most difficult problem in occupational health, and national economies (Bond,2008). The effect of the Psychosocial Work Environment on employees' emotional, physical and mental well-being and their efficiency, effectiveness, and productivity, has been emphasised and acknowledged by numerous national governments over the last few decades.

3.1.3 Various Models of Psychosocial Work Environment

3.1.3.1 Job Demand-Control and Job Demand-Control-Support Models

Karasek is credited with developing the most well-known and widely verified model of stress. The 'job demand-control model,' as it is known, postulates that the relationship between job demands and well-being. According to the model, the jobs that have the greatest negative impact on health combine high demands with little control. Increased job demands are not always harmful, rather, it depends on the level of control over the situation.

Based on this theory, the negative impact of high demand is lessened to a certain extent if job involve a combination,of active job with continuous learning and development.

As an additional component, Karasek and Theorell (1990) expanded their model by including social support in the workplace. Social support was defined as "overall levels of helpful social interaction available on the job from both co-workers and supervisors," according to the new theorization of the JDCS model, a workplace can be described in terms of the combination of demands that are present in the job, the amount of control that employees must manage in order to meet those demands, and the support that they receive from both supervisors and co-workers.

3.1.3.2 The Effort-Reward Imbalance Model

The Effort-Reward Imbalance (ERI) model has received considerable support in recent years. This model shifts the emphasis away from control and toward the reward system (Siegrist, 1996). Siegrist emphasises the importance of the work character as a "critical link between self-regulating functions such as self-esteem and self-efficacy and the social opportunity structure.".

This role provides an opportunity for the individual to perform, be rewarded and honoured, and be a part of an influential group. Social rewards can take the form of esteem, money or status control. Status control is concerned with an individual's perception of job security, advancement prospects, and so forth.

This aspect is considered critical in today's global economy, characterised by job insecurity, redundancy, and forced occupational mobility. The assumption that people would remain unstable with high effort and low reward contradict the value expectancy theory, which assumes rational choice.

These options would assist individuals in striking a balance between energy consumption and gratification. On the other hand, the ERI model assumes that the risk of losing one's job and subsequently falling further down the social ladder outweighs the costs of accepting excessively low compensation. These needs appear to correspond to Maslow's basic level equity theory, which places a premium on a fair return on the employee's contribution,and cornerstone of the ERI model.

Over the last two decades, numerous studies have established that inequity between reward and effort is a predictor of alcohol, smoking, cardiovascular disease and job-related well-being. A fascinating finding is that the ERI model indicates that the stressful aspects of work are distinct from those indicated by the job-demand-control model. This result implies the two mutually reinforcing models (Vegchel et al., 2005; Tsutsumi & Kawakami, 2004).

3.1.3.3 Conservation of Resources Theory

This type of motivation theory is based on the fundamental premise that people seek to obtain, retain, substitute, and protect resources in various ways. One of the fundamental tenants of conservation of resource theory is that stress occurs when individuals suffer resource loss or fail to retain resources after making a significant investment of resources in those resources. As a result of this principle, the process of resource loss, acquisition, and protection serve as the primary explanation for both burnout and engagement at work. The characteristics, personal energies, objects, and conditions that individuals value as resources are those that enable them to acquire other objects, personal characteristics, environmental conditions, or energies.

Resources include social support, job advancement opportunities, the degree to which one participates in decision-making, psychological well-being or an optimistic personality, the degree to which one is autonomous, and the existence of established behaviour outcome contingencies. However, the affective component of Burnout and work engagement is the most important factor to consider. This component is produced by processes that tap into people's inherent energetic resources: their emotional strength, cognitive agility, and physical vigour. Consequently, Burnout occurs due to a process of resource depletion that gradually depletes energetic resources over time. In contrast, engagement occurs due to an inverted process of actual or anticipated resource gain, which increases energetic resources.

3.1.3.4 Job Characteristics Model

Job Characteristics Model (JCM) Work performance, internal motivation, absenteeism and turnover are all improved by three psychological states. These psychological states include experiencing meaning in work done, taking responsibility for work outcomes, and knowing the outcomes of the work done.

Employees will be more engaged in their jobs if they are purposefully designed to be varied and meaningful and if they have ample opportunities for two-way communication. According to Hackman & Oldham, they will also have a greater sense of responsibility for the outcomes of their work activities.

They discovered that in order for employees to be satisfied at their jobs, the following work characteristics must be present:

- Task diversification: “Are the tasks varied and difficult to complete? Or do they come across as boring and simple”?
- “Do they have a distinct beginning, middle, and end when it comes to tasks? It is not easy to experience the satisfaction of a goal that has been achieved without this”.
- Meaning of the job: “Does the individual believe that their job has a purpose”?
- “Is it possible for people to have a say in how they go about their daily lives in their jobs’?
- “Employees are given feedback on their work performance. Do they receive it”?

3.2 Job Burnout

Burnout research has become increasingly important as employers have recognised that many employees in different professions in worldwide suffer from burnout syndrome as one of the most serious disorders in today's work environment.

Burnout syndrome has been discussed for more than 40 years and has already developed into a kind of "epidemic," with ramifications on an individual, organisational, and social level. The body of knowledge about this syndrome has been growing exponentially over the years.

Burnout is a psychological reaction to work-related stress. While Burnout is more prevalent in face-to-face jobs, it is widely accepted as a sign of low well-being (Maslach et al., 2001). This is a form of prolonged occupational stress that manifests as, a loss of energy, emotional exhaustion, and withdrawal from work.

Table 3.2

Definitions of Burnout

Authors	Definitions
Pines and Aronson (1988)	"A condition of physical, emotional, and mental exhaustion produced by prolonged involvement in emotionally draining events."
Freudenberger and Richelson (1980)	"A condition of exhaustion or dissatisfaction caused by devotion to a cause, way of life, or relationship that does not achieve the desired result and ultimately results in a decrease in commitment and effectiveness at work."
Maslach et al. (1986)	"Burnout is a workplace phenomenon that results from an inability to manage persistent working stress effectively. It is characterised by cynicism, exhaustion, and diminished proficient effectiveness".
Maslach and Leither (2016)	"An overwhelming exhaustion, feelings of cynicism and alienation from the job, and a sense of ineffectiveness and lack of success as a result of extended interpersonal pressures at work".
Gil Monte and Peiro (1997)	As a result of "continuous work-related stress, the syndrome manifests as a variety of attitudes and negative feelings against the persons who get our services".

The clinical descriptions of burnout were the first conceptual development stage. An empirical phase followed, during which the emphasis shifted from exploratory research on Burnout to systematic research on Burnout, and particularly on the assessment of Burnout. Finally, in order to integrate the evolving concept of burnout with other conceptual frameworks, an increasing amount of theoretical development has taken place.

3.2.1 Historical Evolution of the Burnout Concept

The initial articles on Burnout appeared in the mid-1970s in the United States (Maslach, 1976; Freudenberger, 1974). These early articles were significant because they provided an initial explanation of the burnout phenomenon, provided it with a term, and demonstrated that it was not an aberrant response reserved for a small number of deviant individuals, but was more common among the general population instead.

Herbert Freudenberger (1974) use the term burnout to describe a general condition of negativity, cynicism, and diminished job interest among co-workers. The term has been part of the popular lexicon culture since its inception (Shepherdet al., 2011).

Freudenberger worked as a psychiatrist in a health care agency. He noticed that many of the volunteers he worked with were gradually depleted emotionally and lost motivation and dedication. This procedure typically took about a year and was associated with a variety of mental and physical symptoms. Freudenberger used a term that was colloquially used to denote to the effects of long-lasting drug misuse to describe this particular mental state of exhaustion: "burnout."

At the same time, Maslach, a social psychology researcher, looked into how people deal with emotional stimulation while at work in his research. "Detached concern," "dehumanisation in self-defence" were some of the cognitive approaches she was interested in. However, she quickly realised that both stimulation and strategy had significant consequences for people's lives and behaviours on the job.

However, Graham Greene's A Burnt-Out Case (1960), a film about a psychologically tortured and disappointed architect who, resigns from his profession and retreats to the African jungle. The signs and indicators of the character's actions fit fairly well with contemporary descriptions of Burnout. Burnout causes ineffective, feeling exhausted, and disconnected from work and society (Maslach & Leiter, 2008).

Maslach et al.,(2001) hypothesised that Burnout occurs solely due to one's work atmosphere. Maslach et al. added that Burnout is caused by emotional strain associated with interpersonal contact, in which one's own needs are prioritised over those of others, resulting in emotional exhaustion.

Burnout is the exhaustion of physical or mental strength due to an individual's inability to balance private and professional demands over an extended period. Employees' emotional depletion and exhaustion result in frustration, a lack of ambition, and a sense of loss (Pines & Aronson, 1988). Because the terms stress and Burnout are often used interchangeably, researchers Maslach and Leiter (1997) and Pines and Aronson (1988).distinguished between the two and determined that Burnout is not the same as stress. On the other hand, stress may be the primary cause of Burnout in some people. Burnout is also defined as a "psychological response to chronic work stress characterised primarily by feelings of disengagement and emotional exhaustion from one's work activities".

In the beginning, research on Burnout was qualitative, with researchers conducting interviews to gather data from human services and health care professionals (Maslach et al., 2001). The researchers hypothesised that Burnout could only occur in the context of the workplace.Maslach and colleagues explained that Burnout is caused by emotional stress related to interpersonal contact in which the demands of others are placed before one's own needs. Burnout can also occur due to unrelieved work stress or from the stress that persists and is not effectively managed.

No one is immune to Burnout, and any person belonging to any profession at any level of the organisational hierarchy can be a victim of Job Burnout. Burnout has become a significant concern in the workplace, as it often results in emotional and physical problems that affect job performance.

Burnout does not occur overnight and usually begins with minor warning signs that are difficult to identify. As a result, the exact cause of Burnout cannot always be pinpointed. Instead, it develops in phases,found Lee and Ashforth (1993) through their longitudinal study on supervisors and managers.

Burnout has negative consequences for the individuals who experience it and the workplace as a whole. In organisations where there is a high level of burden and high employee expectations, incidents of burnout are common. Absenteeism, feelings of hopelessness, sabotage, secrecy, malpractice, low productivity, no-compliance, interference of office politics, failure to meet deadlines, confusion about goal sensitiveness, backstabbing,and interpersonal and group conflict are the some of the antecedent of Job Burnout.

3.2.2 Models of Job Burnout

The primary elements that contribute to Burnout are competitiveness and perceived effectiveness. According to his approach, motivation initially determines a subject's effectiveness in accomplishing work objectives; consequently, the stronger the motivation, the better the job efficiency.

The Maslach Burnout Inventory is based on Maslach and Jackson's (1986) model, which asserts that it occurs under extended work pressure. Burnout can occur person's repeated failure to deal with difficult and demanding situations at work and a loss of resistance to work stress.

Based on this model,burnout is defined by three dimensions that include distinct types of symptoms: emotional exhaustion ("a sense of being overworked and exhausted"), depersonalisation or cynicism ("negative attitudes toward recipients"), and a lack of personal accomplishment or diminished effectiveness. Maslach and Jackson (1986) established the Maslach burnout inventory to examine employees on the three previously described burnout dimensions. Emotional weariness has consistently been recognised as the MBI's core, more stable, and reliable component as it typically manifests first and predicts the other two mechanisms in long term research (Maslach & Schaufeli,1993).

Another model of Job Burnout is defined by Pines and Aronson (1988) is "state of physical, emotional, and mental exhaustion caused by prolonged involvement in emotionally demanding situations." It is a severe impairment of one's ability to cope caused by the chronic presence of extremely high expectations and situational stress. Burnout as a state of physical, emotional, and mental exhaustion characterised by low energy, fatigue,a sense of helplessness and hopelessness, disenchantment and disillusionment with work, the development of a adverse self-concept, and a negative and dehumanising opinion of others in their position.

When it comes to Burnout, according to the Cox, Kuk, and Leiter (1993) model, it is considered to be a specific episode within occupational stress that affects especially human service providers and occurs in settings where coping techniques are ineffective. According to these authors, emotional tiredness is synonymous with "feeling worn out." Depersonalisation is viewed as a coping mechanism in the face of emotional weariness, but sentiments of low personal achievement are associated with the subject's cognitive judgement of their stress experience.

Gil-Monte (1997) asserts that the sense of guilt experienced during the burnout process. One describes workers who do not have significant feelings of guilt and who, despite Burnout, continue to perform their jobs, even if they are of a poorer quality. For others, guilt will result in increased work involvement in an attempt to lessen their sorrow. As long as working conditions remain unchanged, reviving depersonalisation,low levels of personal fulfilment at work and emotional weariness will increase. This vicious circle reintroduces new feelings of guilt or intensifies old ones, creating a feedback loop that promotes burnout syndrome.

The Copenhagen Burnout Inventory (CBI) was established by Kristensen et al (2005) in reaction to the criticism thrown at the concept developed by Maslach and her colleagues. According to CBI theory, Burnout can be broadly defined as a "condition of weariness that is work,client burnout and personal Burnout" (Borritz & Kristensen, 1999). Personal Burnout, the generic component of CBI, is developed for those do not have work, including young people, the jobless, early retirees, housewives , and seniors. Other subscales, questions are phrased in such a way that employees of various professions can respond. As Kristensen et al., (2005) assert, "the three measures can be employed in a variety of contexts (all individuals, individuals who work, and those who perform client work). As a result,in many real research, using only one or two of the scales would be meaningful.

3.3 Turnover Intention

Due to the globalisation of the economy, organisations, regardless of its type or size, faces employee turnover at all levels. It is a significant predictor of actual turnover (Griffeth et al., 2000). While turnover imposes numerous direct and indirect costs on an organisation, it also erodes social capital (Kuria et al.,2012). Employees initiate voluntary turnover, it is the procedure by which an employee voluntarily terminates their employment relationship. On the other hand, with the organisation, involuntary turnover is initiated by the employer (Takase,2010).

Table 3.3

Definitions of Turnover Intention

Authors	Definitions
Tett and Meyer (1993)	The term "intention to leave the organisation" refers to a "conscious and deliberate desire to leave the organisation."
Gustafson (2002)	Turnover is "the ratio of people who resigned from an organisation during a specified period to the average number of workers in the organisation during the same period."
Vandenberg & Nelson (1999)	"Turnover intention is an individual's own estimated probability that they will permanently leave the organisation at some point in the immediate future."
Jacobs & Roodt, (2007)	Generally speaking, turnover intention is a mental decision made by employees about whether or not to remain with the company.
Bigliardi et al., (2005)	"The employee's behaviour that indicates a desire to leave their current position."

The first focus of studies on turnover was on "departure rates" and "employment stability." These studies were done during the turn of the twentieth century, and employee turnover has been a subject of much investigation since then. The issue has grown in popularity over the previous decade, with numerous studies published in important publications of management and related fields (Bakker et al., 2014).

It is vital for businesses to safeguard their employees' well-being and to maintain a low turnover rate. Retaining labour capital is critical in the ever-increasing rivalry in markets for valuable employees (Carmeli & Schaubroeck, 2015). Managers and researchers view turnover as a concern due of the accompanying expenses.Turnover intentions refer to an individual's subjective assessment of the likelihood that she or he will quit the organisation in the near future (Kim & Stoner, 2008).

It is defined as a "deliberate and conscious desire to leave an organisation in the near future, and is considered the final stage of the withdrawal cognition process" (Mobley, 2012), which also includes thoughts of quitting and intentions to look for alternative employment opportunities, whether through a passive or active job search (Tett & Meyer, 2011). According to Bakker et al. (2014), turnover intentions serve as an immediate prelude to turnover behaviour. Identifying the elements that influence turnover intentions is thought to be beneficial in lowering actual turnover levels.

Furthermore, Carmeli and Weisberg (2012) propose that Turnover Intentions comprise three distinct mechanisms of the extraction cognitive process (i.e., thoughts of leaving the job, searching for a different job, and then intention to quit). While the intention to depart is distinct from actual turnover, researchers have established that it has a direct causal effect on employee turnover.

3.4 Underpinning Theoretical Model of the Study

The researcher has undergirded this study with the help of Bakker and Demerouti job demands resource model to understand the effect of Psychosocial Work Environment and its link to Turnover Intention and how Job Burnout mediates these relationships among retail textiles shop salespersons.

3.4.1 Job Demand Resource Model (JD-R Model)

The Job Demand Resource Model was applied as a theoretical framework for this study. The JD-R model is useful for many occupations and organisations and is generally recognised in research regarding workplace stress. It has been suggested to describe how employees' working conditions affect their health, work performance, commitment, and turnover intention (Bakker & Demerouti, 2007).

It has a broad scope that allows for the inclusion of all relevant job characteristics within its area. In contrast to other models, the model allows for considering a wide range of possible working environments, making it applicable to a wide range of occupations. More than other models, it serves as a common communication tool for all stakeholders. This model is extremely popular among academic researchers because it is comprehensive, broad, flexible, and communicative. It is also very suitable for practical application in organisations because of its comprehensive, flexible, and easy to communicate.

According to the description given by Demerouti et al., (2001) the JD-R model, has both demands and resources. Work overload, job insecurity, and interpersonal conflicts are examples of job demands, which are the 'negative things' that sap energy at work. By contrast, job resources are the 'positive things' that are defined as "aspects of the job that may contribute to achieving work goals, reduce job demands, promote personal growth and development." Job resources include assistance from others, job control, and performance feedback.

To put it simply, the JD-R model incorporates two fundamental psychological procedures. First and foremost, a stress response triggered by high job demands and insufficient resources may manifest itself in the form of burnout, low performance, impaired workability, and a lack of organisational commitment. If job demands are consistently high and are not effectively compensated by job resources, an employee's vigor will be gradually depleted. This can eventually lead to a condition of Burnout, which can have significant consequences for the individual, such as ill-health, and for the organisation, such as poor performance and high turnover intentions among employees (Hockey,1997).

The following section of the chapter discusses the selected significant variables and their relationships, which serve as the foundation for this study and conceptual framework. As discussed in this section, the established relationships between the various variables selected for this study and provided direction for articulating the research hypotheses. The conceptual framework is illustrated in figure 3.1

3.5 The Magnitude of the Relations

3.5.1 Psychosocial Work Environment and Job Burnout

A growing body of literatures indicate that the Psychosocial Working Environment directly affects occupational health indices like Job Burnout and Turnover Intention. For example, exposure to negative psychosocial job characteristics causes unfavourable psychophysiological distress, which leads to exhaustion. In addition, psychosocial threats have shown to harm employees' physical, emotional, and mental health (Bonde,2008).

Workplace content and demands, workplace social relationships, workplace organisation, and workplace culture are all variables that can impact employees mental and physical well-being. All these aspects of work are referred to as occupational stressors, and they can affect employees' cognitive, mental, physical, and emotional well-being, and prolonged existence of these stressors leads to Job Burnout. The reasons for the high prevalence of Job Burnout among human service professions were identified by Pines and Aronson (1988). According to them, most people who join the human service field are inspired by a wish to interact with others and make a difference in the lives of persons they serve. These human service workers have high hopes that their attempts to support others will be fruitful. If they do not meet this goal, they are setting themselves up for future Job Burnout. The following section presents the relationship of various Psychosocial Work Environment factors with Job Burnout and Turnover Intention.

3.5.2 Quantitative Demand and Job Burnout

Quantitative Demand is the amount of work that individuals think is expected of them in a short period of time and is operationalised in terms of a fast tempo of labour. Quantitative Demand is a term linked with workload. Workload may denote work time responsibilities such as the number of times spent on work and work-related activities. Time pressure, on the other hand,it is a situation where employees believe they have an excessive number of tasks to complete but not enough time to complete them in a timely manner (Fronea et al., 1997). Thus, it appears as though, the two primary aspects of quantitative demands at work are the intensity of the work pace, also known as work pressure, and extensity, such as the number of working hours (Kristensen et al., 2004).

In order to achieve work objectives and prevent performance from slipping, high Quantitative Demand necessitates the expenditure of additional time and energy. An increase in physical and psychological activation has a negative impact on an employee's physical and psychological well-being, leading to fatigue and irritability. Short-term, the employee may be able to recover by taking a break or engaging in activities that are less physically demanding. Activation that is sustained over a prolonged period of time, on the other hand, makes it increasingly difficult to achieve recovery. When the employee's vigour is depleted due to insufficient recovery, the result is an accumulation of fatigue-related symptoms over a period of time (Eriksen et al., 1999). Consequences of prolonged activation may include a gradual depletion of an employee's physical or mental resources, which may eventually lead to exhaustion. (Demerouti et al., 2001; Bakker & Demerouti, 2007). It has been shown that quantitative workload is associated with role conflict,frustration,and fatigue after a workday ,and Job Burnout (Spector and Jex, 2011; Pisanti et al., 2015).

3.5.3 Emotional Demand and Job Burnout

Emotional Demand is defined as "dealing with strong feelings such as sorrow, anger, desperation and frustration" at work (Briner et al., 2008).Voice-to-voice or face-to-face interaction with other people is typically required in emotionally demanding roles. Employees are likely to show only positive emotions and to keep their true feelings hidden from others. Burnout researchers all agree that excessive Emotional Demands are to blame for the development of Burnout in the first place. Employees who are subjected to high Emotional Demands and conflicting responsibilities are more likely to report psychological suffering, putting them at greater risk of developing mental health disorders as well as being less productive(Johanson et al.,2013). In an emotionally challenging role, employees have to display certain repress emotions and positive behaviour. Additionally,they will be expected to elicit an emotional response in another person. If Emotional Demands are not managed effectively, they can result in depression, disengagement, and Burnout.

Human services workers are subjected to a slew of emotional demands, which is a major contributing factor to their stress and ill-health. Many human service occupations, on the other hand, are inherently demanding, particularly when it comes to emotional requirements.As a result, it is frequently difficult to reduce this particular type of demand (Bakker and Sanz-Vergel, 2013).

3.5.4 Lack of Supervisory Support and Job Burnout

Social support is described as "the subset of individuals in an individual's social network on whom he or she relies for socioemotional support, instrumental support, or both" (Thoits, 1982). The supervisor's support was critical in assisting employees in achieving job satisfaction and avoiding depression. Numerous research on nurses have found that high levels of work support, particularly from the immediate supervisor, are connected with decreased levels of Burnout.

For decades, experts have consistently established that social support is a critical resource since it promotes an individual's physical, psychological, and total well-being.Social support comes from three distinct sources: friends,family, co-workers, and the direct supervisor. Social support is the most effective technique to assist an individual in tolerating the unavoidable difficulties at work. Simply put, it is the assistance or support that an individual can obtain in order to do daily tasks through interactions with their family members, supervisor, co-workers, and society.

Supervisory support denotes that the extent to which employees recognise their supervisor's efforts and are concerned about their well-being. It is measured in percentages (Eisenberger et al.,2002). Workers may benefit from programmes that provide emotional support, which are provided by supervisors who represent a variety of managerial positions (Assistant Managers, General Managers, and so on) (Jordan et al., 2002; George et al., 1993).

However, social support from a supervisor can help to reduce stress levels in salespeople who are particularly vulnerable. Besides providing task-relevant resources, such as technical information and training, supervisors can also show empathy, encourage and recognise employees who have done well in their jobs. Salespeople who receive this type of support are less likely to become overwhelmed and eventually burn out their careers (Cutrona,1986)

Job Demand-Resource (JD-R) theory was used to demonstrate the critical role of social support in preventing job-related Burnout. Burned-out employees are more likely to lose focus on their jobs and make fatal errors, necessitating intervention by the organisation. Employees who have social support are experience less emotional, mental, and physical exhaustion than employees who have a low level of support. According to some studies, social support has a primary or direct effect on Burnout, implying that support can help people avoid Burnout regardless of the severity of work stressors (Beehe, 1985).

If employees do not have enough social support, they will feel burned out. To avoid that, it has been observed that supervisors should recognise and deal with employee concerns, communicate with them, and provide them with necessary information.

Stress can be caused by a lack of supervisor support or by negative leadership; a lack of appreciation and respect, such as being assigned unneeded tasks, can result in the intention to leave the company.

3.5.5 Co-worker Support and Job Burnout

Co-worker support is defined as "the degree to which employees believe their co-workers are willing to provide them with work-related assistance in order to assist them in performing their service-related duties" (Zhou et al., 2001).

According to the research, receiving emotional care in the form of empathy and care from co-workers can significantly assist employees in alleviating emotional exhaustion and reducing depersonalisation (Peerayuth et al., 2016). In addition, co-worker support can help to reduce absenteeism, increase opportunities for employees to learn and apply new attitudes, skills and job satisfaction by fostering a supportive environment in the workplace. As a result, the quality of social support can impact the level of Burnout that employees experience at their place of employment.

3.5.6 Abusive Supervision and Job Burnout

Despite the fact that the majority of leadership research has been on constructive and productive leadership behaviours, recent years have seen an increase in research on abusive or deviant leadership behaviours(Pelletier,2010). According to Tepper (2000), abusive supervision is defined as "subordinates' perceptions of the extent to which their supervisors engage in a sustained display of hostile verbal and nonverbal behaviours, with the exception of physical contact". In addition, abusive supervision is not delimited to insulting and attempting to undermine and public condemnation, aggressive and criticising,unrealistic targets,favouritism, angry outbursts and partiality. For instance, you may come across an abusive supervisor who continues to threaten an employee simply because they disagree with them, or you may come across an abusive supervisor who excludes an employee from information that is critical to their job (Wang et al.,2020).

Having a bad day and becoming angry with an employee would not be considered abusive supervision; continuous exposure must occur in order to be considered abusive supervision (Tepper, 2007). When an employee believes their supervisor's arrogance or incompetence are to blame for the abuse, rather than the organisation (Rogelberg, 2007).

A significant number of studies were conducted in order to understand the consequences of Abusive Supervision. Based on this research, a various of outcomes have been identified related to the effects on employees' attitudes, behaviours, and overall health. Underperformance (Walter et al., 2015) displaced aggressive behaviour (Tepper & Simon, 2015), reduced employee satisfaction (Leary et al., 2013), reduced creative thinking (Liu, Liao, & Loi, 2012), perceived organisational injustice (Tepper, 2000), decreased sharing of knowledge (Choi et al.,2012), and a diminished sense of meaning in work are all examples of such outcomes (Rafferty & Restubog, 2011).

Abusive treatment from supervisor resuls in feelings of worthlessness and exclusion. According to Hobman, Restubog, Bordia, and Tang (2009), they experience low self-worth and reduced self-efficacy as a result of their experiences with the programme (Dirican & Erdil, 2020). It is possible that this will result in decreased performance (Pelletier, 2010), increased hostility, or the adaptation of their own behaviours in an effort to better 'fit in' (Vogel & Mitchell, 2017). While the latter may appear to be beneficial to the employee at first, it can be detrimental to their sense of self, resulting in a negative impact on their psychological well-being. The findings of Rafferty and Restubog (2011) revealed that abused personnel perceived themselves as incompetent and worthless of their jobs, as well as insignificant to the organisation. Furthermore, abusive supervision has been linked to diminished physical well-being, as it has been shown to increase the number of somatic health complaints (Harvey et al., 2007).

Psychologically disengaged employees become physically disengaged and emotionally disconnected from their work. Additional research has established a link between abusive supervision and decreased employee well-being. This abuse can have a negative impact on an employee's psychological and physical health, as well as their job-related health. Abusive Supervision has been linked to an increased anxiety and depression as well as emotional exhaustion leading to Burnout (Breaux et al., 2008; Tepper, 2000).

According to Martinko et al., (2013) Abusive Supervision is related to poor mental health, whereas Breaux et al., (2008) discovered that Abusive Supervision is associated with strain. According to Li et al., (2016), this can result in psychological distress, which can have a negative effect on well-being and life satisfaction. As Ganster and Rosen's (2013) model of stress demonstrates, stressors such as Abusive Supervision can have an effect on a body's immune, cardiovascular, and metabolic systems. The way a leader gives direction, distributes the team's workload, and handles problems has a big impact on the behaviour and well-being of those who follow (Schmid et al., 2018).

Several factors contribute to the depletion of an employee's resources under abusive supervision. First and foremost,it increases the amount of time and effort invested in managing their work,work environment,and abusive supervisor. As a result, they are preoccupied with attempting to prevent the abuse means that they cannot perform at a high level. Second, it diminishes the sense of control that the employee has over their work environment. When a supervisor withholds necessary resources from an employee or denies them the capacity to make choices in their role, the employee may become disengaged. This disinterest has a negative impact on their well-being (Ahmad et al.,2019).

Leaders who adopt negative management styles may create high job demands for their subordinates. High job demands will increase the likelihood the negative consequences of this imbalance. The amount of time and energy required to maintain the working relationship may deplete the employee's resources, resulting in negative outcomes such as Burnout on the part of the employee (Aryee et al., 2015).

3.5.7 Lack of Reward and Recognition and Job Burnout

A'yuninnisa and Saptoto's,(2015) proposed definition "Rewards encompass all monetary, non-monetary, and psychological compensation that an organisation provides its employees in exchange for their work." According to them three major types of employee remuneration are: monetary rewards such as bonuses, a monthly pay check, and financial benefits. Non-monetary rewards such as opportunities for learning and growth, flexible working hours, and interesting work content and psychological rewards such as receiving greetings, recognition, appreciation, and a 'pat on the back.'

Bratton John, and Jeff Gold (2012) developed a reward classification system based on these same three categories. In another study conducted by Mercer (2007), the author identified global drivers of employee engagement: ' recognition and rewards.' Thus, psychological rewards (recognition) are an effective component of a rewarding mix that encourages engagement.

The perception of esteem from colleagues and management and an adequate salary and job security are all considered in the evaluation of reward. High levels of strain and reciprocity between the effort expended and the reward received have been linked to a lack of physical and psychological health. Employees' behaviours, actions, and accomplishments that contribute to the advancement of the organisation toward the business goals established by management are motivated by rewards that are strategically aligned with those goals.

Often all that an employee has required to be recognised for the effort they have put forth. It could take the form of awards, evaluations, bonuses, public praise, or even a prize to achieve this. All of these things contribute to maintaining high morale. On the other hand, if employees believe that their efforts are not being recognised, they are more likely to become demotivated, leading to Burnout and other problems.

3.5.8 Job Insecurity and Job Burnout

According to Sverke et al.,(2002),Job insecurity, is a "subjective experience of involuntary job loss that is associated with feelings of powerlessness and helplessness on the worker's part".Makes a distinction between cognitive and affective insecurity in the workplace. Job insecurity is classified as cognitive or affective. Cognitive job insecurity refers to the perceived chance of job loss, whereas affective job insecurity is the fear of actually losing one's job (Borg & Elizur, 1992).

According to Abolade (2018), Job Insecurity, is an employee's perception of a possible threat to their current job. Job Insecurity, more precisely, is a persistent occupational stressor that has an effect on an employee's well-being.

Job Insecurity is likely to contribute to Burnout and decreased work engagement, as it undermines the concept of reciprocity, which is critical for well-being (Maslach et al.,2001).

Job uncertainty was also associated with poor physical and mental health, decreased self-esteem, decreased life satisfaction, and an increased risk of Burnout. Furthermore, job insecurity harms people's attitudes about work, lowering job engagement, motivation and increasing anxiety and Burnout. Moreover, job insecurity is a stressor that has been linked to higher degrees of Burnout (De Witte., 2005).

Employment insecurity is defined as the "employee's perception of a threat to the continuation of their current job" (De Witte,2005); as seen from this definition, job insecurity is not the same as job loss. When a person loses a job, they try to cope with the loss and problems. Even when the individual does not experience a job loss in the situation of job insecurity (Sverke et al.,2002), the thought of becoming unemployed is stressful. It may assist in comprehending the negative consequences that uncertainty can have on a person's health and well-being.

Burnout syndrome is one of the most severe consequences of job uncertainty for individuals (Bosman et al.,2005). Burnout occurs when employees cannot cope with their working conditions and become oblivious to their surroundings (Maslach et al.,2001). Employees nowadays confront considerable challenges when businesses undergo significant changes such as downsizing, restructuring, and having to deal with flexible work arrangements. Furthermore, as the traditional notion of career strategy has changed, career management is no longer employers' job; instead, workers are responsible for managing their careers. Under those conditions, they are more likely to develop burnout syndrome (Mauno et al.,2005).

3.5.9 Work-Family Conflict and Job Burnout

According to Greenhaus and Beutell (1985) work-family conflict is a "type of role conflict in which the demands of the work and family domains are mutually incompatible in some way". Work-family matters have grown in importance for workers, families, and organisations (Bourhis & Mekkaoui, 2010). Less time is available for family responsibilities and obligations, stress on the home-work interfaces has increased (Slan-Jerusalim & Chen, 2009). Consequences of long work hours and the effort to balance work and family life are a recurring theme in the literature (Slan-Jerusalim & Chen, 2009; Aluko, 2009) Major, Klein, and Ehrhart (2002) stated in their research that "extended work hours are associated with increased work–family conflict and, at least indirectly, psychological distress".

Although not new, the work-family conflict topic has gained increased attention in the Personal Sales field throughout the years as it has been identified as one of the five emerging psychosocial risks in today's working environment (Bande et al., 2019). It will be, therefore, quickly established that the repercussions of this type of occurrence will be of an individual nature, but also organisational in so far as it leads to important negative consequences for the organisations as well as may lead to significant costs (Carballo et al., 2018) and competitive loss.

It is unquestionable that work-family conflict is an important factor in inducing behavioural shifts of individuals, affecting an individual's well-being and health (Tabassum et al., 2017) and overall life quality.

In general, time constraints and allied factors (e.g., working parents) have resulted in an increased focus on work-family conflict and its related outcomes in research. It is well known that conflict occurs either in the workplace and extends into the home or in the home and extends into the workplace. This bidirectional strategy for resolving conflict is well recognised (Warner & Hausdorf, 2009).

According to studies on work-family conflict and psychological well-being, when work-related well-being factors are considered, work-family conflict is associated with job stress, Burnout, and decreased job satisfaction.

Work and family are most important domains for many employees. In an ideal world, they would work for hand in hand and not interfere with one another, causing problems. But this is not the case for all individuals. Problems in one domain can sometimes spill over into the other domain, resulting in conflict between work and family life (Howard et al., 2004). Work-family conflict is a type of inter-role conflict in which the role pressures from the work and family domains are mutually incompatible in some way. In other words, participation in the family (work) role exacerbates the difficulty of participation in the work (family) role. In other words, excessive job demands make it more difficult for people to recover sufficiently at home due to the amount of effort they have put in at their place of employment. It implies that there is a high possibility that excessive work demands will have a negative influence on psychological health and result in job burnout (Greenhaus and Beutell,2006).

3.5.10 Customer Incivility and Job Burnout

Customers' incivility is defined as rude behaviour on the part of customers who violate social norms, are disrespectful of one another, and who hurt employees who provide services, despite the fact that they do not show it. These behaviours include irritating employees who serve and their customers by talking about them, complaining about slow service, and failing to express gratitude to the employees for their service. It's also important to note that they treat service employees with contempt (Zhu et al.,2019).

It is possible to become physically and mentally exhausted as a result of customers' rudeness (Han,Bonn, & Cho2016). When customers' servants are emotionally exhausted, they experience feelings of helplessness, hopelessness, and weakness, which leads to incivility in their interactions with them.

3.6 Psychosocial Work Environment and Turnover Intention

The advancement of human resource management has resulted in a call for greater attention to be paid to the policies that organisations impose on their employees. Policies that do not align with the needs and expectations of employees will have an adverse impact on their work attitudes. Numerous studies have established that employees with a positive work attitude are more productive than those with a negative work attitude. Employees who exhibit a favourable attitude toward their jobs will have lower absenteeism and turnover intention than their counterparts (Hartati.,1992). The presence of a poor working environment, insufficient wages, excessive working hours, and the absence of social security benefits are the most common reasons for employees' intention to quit their jobs. Poor working conditions have been linked to a higher likelihood of leaving, according to research. If employers do not take the necessary steps to improve working conditions, workers are less likely to abandon their plans to leave their current employers (Cottini et al., 2011)

3.6.1 Quantitative Demand and Turnover Intention

Quantitative demand refers to work that needs excessive effort and speed, as well as time constraints and contradictory demands. Work overload has a number of negative consequences for the organisation, including the potential loss of employees, as many employees who experience Burnout eventually leave their jobs, as well as less-than-optimal work that is marked by errors and represents a drain on the organisation's resources (Moodie et al., 2014). Additionally, research indicates high workloads have a detrimental effect on employees' job performance.Many employees who are burnt out due to job overload perform at a very low level. Similarly,increased workload resulted in an increase in turnover intentions (Michelle,2013).

3.6.2 Emotional Demand and Turnover Intention

Long working hours, lack of social support, abusive supervision, working shifts, and physical/psychological exertion contribute to job strain and overburdening of the role. When employees perceive that the demands of their jobs have turned into a pressure that exceeds their capacity to resolve, the employees will be subjected to excessive stress and may even consider quitting their jobs in the organisation. As a result, job demands can cause employees to experience work stress and reduced job satisfaction, which can lead to employees leaving the organisation (Robbins & Judge, 2013).

Employee emotional demand is another critical factor to consider when discussing employee turnover. The emotional demand of employees is defined by Johannessen, Tynes, and Sterud (2013) as coping with strong emotions such as sorrow, anger, desperation, and frustration at work. Additionally, the study discovered that "role conflict and emotional demand are the most significant risk factors for psychological distress in workers, which has been associated with decreased job productivity and absenteeism."Futhermore, it is an emotionally charged workplace interaction that is a significant source of job strain.

3.6.3 Lack of Supervisory Support and Turnover Intention

When employees believe that their employer supports them, they work harder and achieve higher levels of success in their positions. Those who do not feel supported, on the other hand, may adopt an inactive attitude toward their effort and may experience Burnout, which will reduce their productivity. A supportive work environment is critical in reducing various job stressors as well as improving job performance. As a result, social support can help to reduce employee Job Burnout and Turnover Intentions (Tian et al., 2014).

3.6.4 Co-worker Support and Turnover Intention

Co-workers' significance is predicated on a relational view of turnover According to the relational perspective, organisations suffer negative consequences as a result of low-quality interpersonal relationships, including high employee turnover. Positive outcomes, on the other hand, such as increased employee retention, are associated with high-quality interpersonal relationships.When employees are confronted with negative aspects of the work environment, positive interpersonal relationships act as a buffer, aiding in employee retention. According to Mossholder et al.,(2005) as individuals develop more extensive, high-quality relationships, their attachment to and integration into the organisation grows. Surprisingly, research to date has not conclusively established that co-worker support decreases turnover. While the relational perspective implies that co-worker support is critical for reducing turnover, empirical evidence is mixed. Co-workers have been shown to have a significant impact on employee intentions to leave and actual turnover behaviour in previous research (Ng and Sorensen,2008).

3.6.5 Abusive Supervision and Turnover Intention

Abusive supervision is the primary reason why people dislike their supervisor and job. Turnover is also associated with abusive supervision. Existing literature models provide rationales for the proposition that increasing levels of abusive supervision will increase intentions to leave (Tepper, 2000). If this interaction relationship becomes strained due to the supervisor's abusive behaviour, several negative consequences may occur, with subordinates' decision to quit the organisation (Waldman et al., 2004). In the case of subordinates who believe their supervisor is abusive, the embarrassment and undermining they receive will be viewed as "unfair." Harris and colleagues (2007) found that the victimised employee either engaged in deviant behaviour in response to the abuses or considered leaving the organisation as a result of their experiences.According to Porter and Steers (1973) "met expectations" theory employees typically expect to have a positive relationship with their supervisor, but if this expectation is not met, and the employee has a dissatisfying relationship with the supervisor, the dissatisfied employee may plan to leave his or her company as a result of the unmet job expectation.

The evidence has shown that abusive supervision leads to decreased job satisfaction, excessive stress, absenteeism, and turnover on a professional level (Schmid et al., 2018).

3.6.6 lack of Reward and Recognition and Turnover Intention

A'yuninnisa and Saptoto (2015) postulated that the salary level has a stronger relationship with the intention to leave than other aspects such as commitment and job satisfaction. This finding indicates that the income level is more important in terms of turnover intention, as noted in the desire of employees to leave the company and look for another opportunity. Furthermore, a lack of equitable rewards and recognition systems may result in an unsatisfactory workforce within the organisation, as today's employees expect to be treated as valuable resources rather than disposable assets. Consequently, in the current environment, retention of qualified and skilful employees within organisations has emerged as one of the most common challenges. As a result of this, one of the most critical problems that managers of organisations face today is the intention and execution of employee turnover (Agarwal., 2010).

3.6.7 Job Insecurity and Turnover Intention

Employees who feel unsafe at work are more likely to leave. When employees are dissatisfied and insecure, their psychosocial health suffers and their intention to leave increases (Hur & Perry., 2014). When a company's employees experience a high level of job insecurity, job satisfaction suffers and the likelihood of employee turnover increases.

Job insecurity is a psychological state in which an employee feels threatened or concerned about his or her future employment. Employees who are concerned or nervous on the job will develop an unpleasant attitude toward their jobs, contributing to their dissatisfaction with their jobs and desire to leave the company

If employees continue to face job insecurity, it can result in the emergence of a desire to move or turnover intentions.If the number of employees experiencing job insecurity increases as a result of their employment status as a contract employee, it can result in a high turnover intention among a company's employees(Arijanto et al., 2020).

3.6.8 Work-Family Conflict and Turnover Intention

Cohen (1997) proposed that work-family conflict could lead to employees quitting their jobs because the high tasks and stress that accumulate in the workplace lead to frustration in the workplace, and frustration at home in the family domain. Employees find it difficult to zone out when not at work and regulate their behaviour and emotions in the short time separates the two locations. As a result, the emotions experienced at work are experienced at home (Greenhaus& Powell, 2006). Furthermore, when employees are at home, they may find it difficult to forget about the work that needs to be completed in the "workplace".

3.6.9 Customer Incivility and Turnover Intention

According to the Conservation of Resource (COR) Theory, the degree of relationship between a customer's negative behaviour and employee turnover is dependent on the degree of resource or gain available to the employee. When an asset is lost, such as when an emotional asset is lost, the worker will experience a high level of emotional exhaustion and may intend or attempt to withdraw from the workplace.

As stated by the COR theory, customer incivility can potentially lower employees' assets such as resourcefulness, confidence, and vitality when it is a source of stress at work (Han et al., 2016). Employees who are subjected to the damaging effects of asset loss may experience mental pressure or Burnout (Hobfoll & Freedy,1993), and those who are subjected to these stresses for an extended period of time are more likely to consider leaving their jobs.

3.7 Job Burnout and Turnover Intention

Jackson et al., (1986) discovered that Burnout is associated with subsequent thoughts of leaving. Salesperson burnout is a multidimensional process that decreases salespersons' performance, job satisfaction, and organisational commitment (Babakus et al.,1999) while increasing salesperson turnover intentions (Boles et al., 1997). It has been shown that retail environment is associated with critical job outcomes such as job satisfaction and stress in empirical studies (Singh & Loncer,2010).

Burnout has been linked to various forms of job withdrawal; these distinct forms of job withdrawal include both the actual turnover and intention to leave (Leiter Michael & Maslach, 2009).

Previous studies shows that employees with a high degree of Burnout in varied fields are more likely to intend to leave (Shimizu et al., 2005). Additionally, organisational research demonstrates a positive relationship between Burnout and turnover.

3.7.1 Emotional Exhaustion and Turnover Intention

Emotional exhaustion refers to the degree to which employees feel emotionally drained and overwhelmed by their work (Leiter & Maslach, 1988). Employees who become emotionally exhausted report feeling "a lack of energy and the sense that their emotional resources have been depleted" (Cordes & Dougherty, 1993).

Emotional exhaustion is the primary element of Burnout because it is a state of exhaustion and fatigue (Halbesleben & Bowler, 2007). The consequences of emotional exhaustion can be detrimental especially in the service industry, where employees are expected to perform at a high level.

Emotional exhaustion is defined by a feeling of being drained, stretched beyond capacity, and depleted of resources. Employees become emotionally exhausted as a result of a scarcity of personal resources. Emotional exhaustion is a state of physical and psychological exhaustion that is prevalent in today's high-stress workplace. Emotional exhaustion refers to behaviours that act as an emotional and cognitive diversion from work.

This high-stress work environment has been linked to increased employee distress (Adams & Webster, 2013), job-specific and psychological strain (Wilson & Holmvall, 2013), emotional exhaustion (van Jaarsveld et al., 2010; Kern & Grandey, 2009), and high employee turnover rates.

3.7.2 Mental Exhaustion and Turnover Intention

Mental weariness can occur in anyone who has been subjected to prolonged stress. It might leave you feeling stressed and emotionally drained, making duties and problems appear insurmountable. Detachment and apathy may wreak havoc on every part of an employee's personal and professional life. Employees may feel stuck in a job where they have no power.

Mental weariness is frequently caused by prolonged stress. Although the term "mental exhaustion" is frequently used to refer to being overworked or to workplace stress, mental exhaustion can also be caused by a prolonged period of persistent stress (Moore, 2000). Mental exhaustion is the result of the combination of two energies, emotional and mental, that are required to meet job demands. Degradation of this energy results in a high sensation of intention to leave among employees.

3.7.3 Physical Exhaustion and Turnover Intention

Chronic fatigue, weakness, low energy, and weariness are all symptoms of physical exhaustion. Accident proneness, illness vulnerability, frequent headaches, pains in various body parts, nausea, and changes in consumption habits and weight are all symptoms. One cause of Burnout is physical exhaustion caused by work. For instance, extreme activity in nature requires ongoing energy to stay concentrated, leading to physical exhaustion. Physical tiredness is a state of excessive exhaustion that leaves one physically exhausted (Cheng & Hu,2010).

3.8 Mediating Role of Job Burnout

Schaufeli and Bakker (2004) discovered that Burnout acts as a mediator between job demands and job resources and the intention to leave a job. Job Burnout is a mediator that has been extensively researched in the context of the JD-R model. There have been numerous studies that link job burnout to a variety of negative consequences in the workplace. Because of the long-term presence of a stressful work environment, it is a highly effective response syndrome to be aware of. When an employee is experiencing Burnout, what started out as a positive, energetic, and productive relationship with their job gradually deteriorates into disengagement, a lack of productivity, and eventually a strong sense of intention to quit. According to Tett and Meyer, turnover is defined as a "conscious and deliberate willingness to leave an organisation, and it is one of the most significant predictors of actual turnover." The experience of job burnout is associated with a variety of negative organisational outcomes, including decreased job performance, absenteeism, job dissatisfaction, and the intention to leave the company. One of the most significant of these consequences is that turnover intention is one of the best predictors of actual turnover (Llorens et al., 2007).

Burnout is critical in determining the impact of role stressors on salespeople's intentions to quit their jobs, according to research (Hunsaker 1986). In a particular role, a variety of sources of stress are frequently present, including long work hours, emotional demands, overload, and a lack of supportive colleagues and peers. Each of these role stressors may or may not be harmful to an individual's health or well-being, but the cumulative effect of these stressors can deplete an individual's coping resources, ultimately leading to Burnout. Salespeople may experience significant dysfunction when multiple role stressors act simultaneously on them. While individual stressors may have a moderate to low impact, it is possible that the cumulative effect is significantly negative. Job outcomes are likely to be moderate or weak in such situations, but the burnout pathway is likely to be strong. The magnitude of role stressors is immaterial; what matters is the magnitude of role stressors in relation to an individual's available coping resources (Jackson et al.,1986). This distinction is critical because certain types of role stress can aid in the creative management of role demands and may even increase productivity when done correctly (Veninga., & Spradley., 1981). As a result, reducing or eliminating role stress may have a negative impact on creativity and overall productivity. Individuals who experience Burnout are those who have exhausted their coping mechanisms and are unable to cope with their role stress any more effectively. As a result, Burnout provides empirical support for the relationship between job stressors and job outcomes that has been hypothesised.

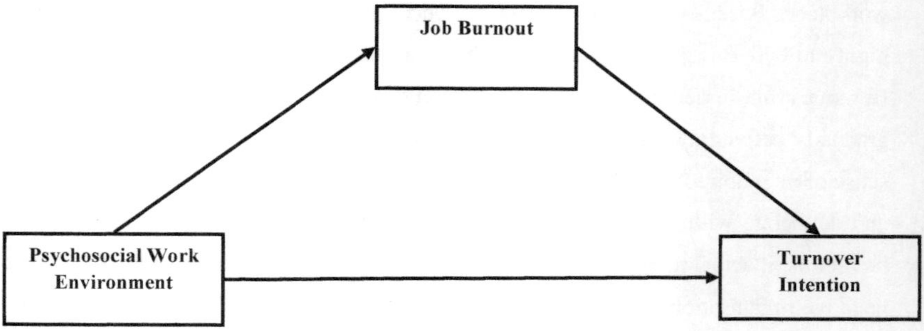

Figure 3.1: Proposed Conceptual Framework of the Study

3.9 Summary of the Chapter

The study proposes that the intensity of the risk factors involved in the Psychosocial Work Environment increases Turnover Intention among retail textile shop salespersons. This study also hypothesised that Job Burnout mediates the relationship between Psychosocial Work Environment and Turnover Intention. The proposed conceptual framework of the study is shown in figure 3.1.

CHAPTER 4

DATA ANALYSIS & DISCUSSION

This chapter begins with the specifics of the sample distribution, including district- and circle-level information and demographic characteristics such as Age, Gender, Marital Status, Educational Qualification, Income, and Work Experience. Then, descriptive statistics were used to describe and summarise the properties of data collected from the respondents. This chapter also explains normality, reliability, and factor analysis before moving on to detailed data analysis. Finally, the structural equation modelling and hypotheses testing were explained, followed by a summary of the hypothesis's findings.

4.1 Sample Profile Characteristics

This section analyses demographic data of 398 salespersons in the retail textile shop in Kerala to understand the influences of Psychosocial Work Environment, Job Burnout, and Turnover Intention. Understanding the demographic characteristics will allow organisations to allocate better resources and efforts to reduce risk factors in the Psychosocial Work Environment and Job Burnout among their employees and combat its adverse effects such as Turnover Intention. This study considers specific demographic data, i.e., Age, Marital Status, Gender, Education, Monthly Income, Years of Experience in the sales profession. The obtained results enhance the knowledge about psychosocial hazards and Job Burnout in the sales profession. The following Table gives the profile characteristics of the salespersons.

4.1.1 District

Table 4.1

District-wise Distribution of the Salespersons

District	Frequency	Per cent
Ernakulam	172	43.2
Calicut	119	29.9
Trivandrum	107	26.9
Total	398	100.0

***Note*:** Computed from Primary Data

The district-wise distribution of the salesperson is shown in Table 4.1. Ernakulam district has the highest population of salespersons, which is at 43.2 per cent. Therefore, the number of retail textiles shops and the total number of salespersons working in the retail textile shops is more in Ernakulam district than in another district—followed by Calicut with 29.9 per cent and Trivandrum district with 26.9 per cent.

4.1.2 Circle

Table 4.2

Circle-wise Distribution of the Salespersons

Circle	Frequency	Per cent
Ernakulam (circle 1)	93	23.4
Ernakulam (circle 2)	79	19.8
Calicut (circle 1)	58	14.6
Calicut (circle 2)	61	15.3
Trivandrum (circle 1)	30	7.5
Trivandrum (circle 2)	77	19.3
Total	398	100.0

Note: Computed from Primary Data

Table 4.2 displays that 23.4 per cent of the salespersons are from Ernakulam Circle 1. From Circle 2, 19.8 per cent of response was collected. 14.6 and 15.3 per cent are from Calicut Circle 1 and Circle 2, respectively. Furthermore, 7.5 per cent are from Trivandrum circle 1, and 19.3 per cent are from Circle 2.

4.1.3 Age

Table 4.3
Age Profile of the Salespersons

Age	Frequency	Per cent
<20	29	7.3
20-30	233	58.5
30-40	95	23.9
40-50	32	8.0
>50	9	2.3
Total	398	100.0

Note: Computed from Primary Data

Table 4.3 observed the Age profile of the salespersons shows that most salespersons come under the Age group of 20-30. Further, only 2.3 per cent of respondents are in the Age group above 50. This supports the findings of Diana Purba et al. (2019).

4.1.4 Gender

Table 4.4
Gender-wise classification of the Salespersons

Gender	Frequency	Per cent
Male	171	43.0
Female	227	57.0
Total	398	100.0

Note: Computed from Primary Data

Table 4.4 displays the Gender-wise classification of the Salespersons. Most of the salespersons are female (57.0 per cent), while males are 43 per cent.

The retail workforce differs from the general workforce in that it employs a higher number of women (Sparks, 1992; Brockbank and Airey, 1994). Women predominate in the retail industry (Pilcher, 2007). According to numerous studies, women are better suited to retail service roles than men (Sirianni &Negrey, 2000; Pettinger (2005).

4.1.5 Marital Status

Table 4.5

Marital Status of the Salespersons

Marital status	Frequency	Per cent
Married	239	60.1
Unmarried	159	39.9
Total	398	100.0

***Note*:** Computed from Primary Data

Table 4.5 depicts that most of the salespersons were married (60.1 per cent), and the remaining 39.9 per cent of salespersons were unmarried. Previous studies findings like Bradley and Brown (2008); Bu and McKeen (2001); Ngo (2002); Warren (2004) show that married salespersons are more per cent than unmarried.

4.1.6 Educational Qualification

Table 4.6

Educational Qualification of the Salespersons

Educational Qualification	Frequency	Per cent
Up to high school	151	37.9
Up to higher secondary	144	36.2
Diploma	22	5.5
Graduation	81	20.4
Total	398	100.0

***Note*:** Computed from Primary Data

The Educational Qualification of most of the salespersons is high school level (37.9 per cent). 36.2 per cent of the salespersons were up to higher secondary. 20.4 per cent of the salesperson has completed graduation.

4.1.7 Monthly Income

Table 4.7

Monthly Income of the Salespersons

Income	Frequency	Per cent
<10000	82	20.6
10000- 15000	239	60.1
15000- 20000	61	15.3
>20000	16	4.0
Total	398	100.0

Note: Computed from Primary Data

Most of the salespersons come under the income group of ₹10000-15000 (60.1 per cent), and only 4 per cent of the salesperson's monthly income above ₹20000. On the other hand, 20.6 per cent of salespersons earn below ₹10000. Therefore, most salespersons are getting an income between ₹ 10000 – 15000.

4.1.8 Working Hours

Table 4.8

Working Hours per day of the Salespersons

Working hours	Frequency	Per cent
9 -10	18	4.5
10 - 11	185	46.5
11 - 12	195	49.0
Total	398	100.0

Note: Computed from Primary Data

As per the Shop and Commercial Establishment Act1960, working hour is 8 hours, but most salespersons have to work 11 - 12 hours (49 per cent). This result is in correspondence with Shabnam et al. (2008).

4.1.9 Work Experience

Table 4.9

Work Experience of the Salespersons

Work experience	Frequency	Per cent
1-5	148	37.2
5-10	161	40.5
10-15	50	12.6
15-20	39	9.8
Total	398	100.0

***Note*:** Computed from Primary Data

Table 4.9 shows that 9.8 per cent of the salespersons have 15-20 years of experience, and 37.2 per cent have 1-5 years of experience.

4.2 Multivariate Data Analysis

Testing multivariate procedures' underlying assumptions is essential to avoid drawing incorrect conclusions. Therefore, the researcher examined the dataset for exploratory factor analysis, normality, reliability, and confirmatory factor analysis in this regard.

4.3 Exploratory Factor Analysis (EFA)

The EFA approach is a well-established method for scale refinement. It entails the following steps: identifying relevant items from the literature, designing a survey instrument to measure these items, conducting a survey, and conducting EFA to recognize the major factors based on the item factor loading. It is a data-driven technique for determining the underlying factors or latent variables related with a set of variables.

Various statistical analyses were applied to determine the appropriateness of the data for exploratory factor analysis, including Kaiser-Meyer-Olkin (KMO) - a measure of sampling suitability - and Bartlett's test of sphericity.

Table 4.10

Results of KMO and Barlett's Test of Sphericity

Variables	No of Variables	Kaiser-Meyer-Oklin Measure of Sampling Adequacy	Bartlett's Test of Sphericity -Chi	df	Sig.
Psychosocial Work Environment	34	0.960	17521.424	561	<0.001***
Job Burnout	21	0.962	19352.107	210	<0.001***

***Note*:** Computed from Primary Data

Kaiser-Meyer-Olkin (KMO) coefficients quantify the degree of correlation between variables. The KMO index is a numeric value between 0 and 1. KMO value of less than 0.50 is deemed unacceptable for factor analysis. The KMO values obtained in this study are 0.960 and 0.962, indicating that the sample size is adequate and the data are suitable for factor analysis (Malhotra, 2008).

The correlation matrix was examined, and it was discovered that several coefficients were between 0.3 and 0.5. As a result, the Kaiser-Meyer-Oklin value was greater than 0.6, above the recommended value of 0.6, and the Barlett's Test of Sphericity gained statistical significance, indicating that the correlation matrix is factorable.

The Bartlett's test result and KMO value shows that the data is suitable for factor analysis, and hence the data can be used to extract the factors. The results are shown in Table 4.10.

After establishing the appropriateness of the data using determinant value, KMO and Barlett's Test of Sphericity, Exploratory Factor Analysis was executed with 34 items of Psychosocial Work Environment 21 items of Job Burnout measures to group the variables. Principal Component Analysis (PCA) was used to analyse the items of all the variables in this study. Prior to performing PCA, it was determined whether or not the data was suitable for factor analysis. The following table gives the classification of the variables based on the factor loading.

Table 4.11

Exploratory Factor Analysis- Psychosocial Work Environment

Factor	Code	Statements	Factor loading
Factor1	QD1	"Do you feel that your hours of work are long"?	0.610
	QD2	"Do you feel any difficulties to keeping your energy level at a high pace throughout the day?"	0.524
	QD3	"Do you have frustration to work like standing for a long time"?	0.713
	QD4	"Do you get sufficient breaks during working hours"?	0.688
Factor 2	ED1	"You are required to be kind and open towards everyone – regardless of how they behave towards you"?	0.867
	ED2	"Do you have to control your emotions"	0.688
	ED3	"Did work put you in emotionally disturbing situations"?	0.827
Factor 3	SsCoW1	"During work time, do you get support and help from your co-workers"?	0.859
	SsCoW2	"Sales targets create competition among co-workers"	0.907
	SsCoW3	"Get support from your co-workers to talk to your supervisors about your work-related problems	0.544
Factor 4	LSsSu1	The immediate supervisor is always willing to solve your work-related problems"?	0.713
	LSsSu2	"Encouraging and Supportive"	0.905
	LSsSu3	"How often does your nearest superior talk with you about how well you carry out your work"?	0.901
Factor 5	AS1	My supervisor scolds me in front of others	0.851
	AS2	"Excessive criticism"	0.863
	AS3	"Doesn't allow me to interact with co-workers"	0.887
	AS4	"Excessive monitoring of work"	0.877
	AS5	"Is rude to me"	0.892
Factor 6	JI1	"Stability of my job is poor"?	0.735
	JI2	"Are you worried about becoming unemployed"?	0.724
	JI3	"Is it difficult for you to find another job if you become unemployed"?	0.825

Factor 7	LReRe1	"I am getting a fair reward for the effort I put into my work"?	0.578
	LReRe2	"Is your work recognized and appreciated by the management"?	0.621
	LReRe3	"Do you get any job promotions like a supervisor, floor manager, etc".?	0.803
	LReRe4	"Are you treated fairly at your workplace"?	0.816
Factor 8	WFC1	"Personal relationships with family members"	0.823
	WFC2	"Your mental and physical state at home"	0.801
	WFC3	"Your participation in in-home activities"	0.844
	WFC4	"Your social life"	0.821
Factor 9	CI1	"Does the customer vent their bad mood on you"?	0.815
	CI2	"Customers consider you as an object"	0.805
	CI3	"Most of the time I get good customers"	-0.661
	CI4	"Customers treat me with dignity"	-0.793
	CI5	"Interacting with customers is a stress relief for me"	-0.799

Method of Extraction: Principal Component Analysis.

Note: Abbreviations- QD= Quantitative Demand; ED= Emotional Demand; SsCoW= Social Support from Co-worker; LSsSu= Lack of Social Support from Supervisor; AS= Abusive Supervision; JI= Job Insecurity; LReRe= Lack of Reward and Recognition; WFC= Work Family Conflict; CI= Customer Incivility.

Principal Component Analysis (PCA) was done on 34 items. All items with a factor loading of greater than 0.5 were kept for further analysis since loading greater than 0.5 was considered fundamentally significant (Hair et al., 2010). The factor loading should be more than 0.5 to keep the items. The factor loadings for the total 34 items ranged from 0.5 to 0.907. Therefore, they were all kept after Exploratory Factor Analysis.

Table 4.12
Burnout measures

Factor	Code	Statements	Factor loading
Factor1	EE1	"Feeling depressed"	0.722
	EE2	"Being emotionally exhausted"	0.722
	EE3	"Feeling burned out"	0.719
	EE4	"Feeling worthless"	0.784
	EE5	"Being troubled"	0.758
	EE6	"Feeling hopeless"	0.770
	EE7	"Feeling anxious"	0.763
Factor 2	ME1	"Having a good day"	0.665
	ME2	"Being happy"	0.663
	ME3	"Being unhappy"	0.608
	ME4	"Feeling trapped"	0.818
	ME5	"Feeling disillusioned and resentful about people"	0.817
	ME6	"Feeling rejected"	0.806
	ME7	"Feeling optimistic"	0.772
Factor 3	PE1	"Being tired"	0.760
	PE2	"Being physically exhausted"	0.806
	PE3	"Being 'wiped out"	0.680
	PE4	"Feeling rundown"	0.660
	PE5	"Being weary"	0.600
	PE6	"Feeling week"	0.584
	PE7	"Feeling energetic"	0.690

Method of Extraction: Principal Component Analysis.
Note: Abbreviations- EE= Emotional Exhaustion; ME= Mental Exhaustion; PE= Physical Exhaustion

Principal Component Analysis (PCA) was done on 21 items. Those items with factor loadings of more than 0.5 were kept for further analysis since loadings greater than0.5 were considered fundamentally significant (Hair et al., 2010). The factor loadings for the full set of 21 items ranged from 0.584 to 0.818. Therefore, they were all kept after Exploratory Factor Analysis.

4.4 Normality

Normality is a term that denotes the degree to which the distribution of sample data resembles a normal distribution (Hair et al., 2014). Multivariate normality is a critical premise underlying multivariate statistical procedures. Multivariate normality explains why each variable and all linear groupings of the variables are assumed to be normally distributed. This assumption confirms the residuals of the analysis. And are also normally and independently distributed (Tabachnick & Fidell 2001).

On the other hand, a value of 0.05 indicates that the variable's distribution deviates significantly from the normal distribution. As shown in Table 4.13, a Kolmogorov-Smirnov value greater than the significant value confirmed the data's normality. Multivariate normality is a critical premise underlying multivariate statistical procedures. Multivariate normality explains why each variable and all linear combinations of the variables are assumed to be normally distributed. This assumption confirms that the analysis's residuals are also normally distributed and independently distributed (Tabachnick & Fidell 2001). To ensure that the normality assumption was not violated in this study, the Kolmogorov-Smirnov test was used to test the null hypothesis that a sample is drawn from a (i.e., normal) distribution. A significance level greater than 0.05 indicates the normally distributed sample data. On the other hand, a value of 0.05 indicates that the variable's distribution deviates significantly from the normal distribution. As shown in Table 4.13, a Kolmogorov-Smirnov value greater than the significant value confirmed the data's normality.

Table 4.13
Kolmogorov – Smirnov Test for Normality

Variables	N	Mean	Std. Deviation	Kolmogorov-Smirnov	p value
Quantitative Demand	398	12.63	4.08	1.398	0.081
Emotional Demand	398	8.21	3.48	1.116	0.133
Social Support from Co-worker	398	6.95	3.40	1.230	0.110
Lack of Social Support from Supervisor	398	8.01	3.75	1.373	0.085
Abusive Supervision	398	12.01	7.00	1.169	0.122
Job Insecurity	398	8.59	4.50	0.353	0.362
Lack of Reward and Recognition	398	10.89	5.18	1.170	0.121
Work-Family Conflicts	398	12.19	4.55	1.210	0.114
"Emotional Exhaustion"	398	16.41	11.31	1.080	0.140
"Mental Exhaustion"	398	18.63	9.53	1.242	0.107
"Physical Exhaustion"	398	18.28	10.08	0.079	0.468
"Turnover Intention"	398	18.85	6.29	1.613	0.054

***Note*:** Computed from Primary Data

4.5 Reliability

Reliability test was conducted to determine the internal consistency of the measurement tools in question. Calculating the coefficient alpha test, also known as Cronbach's alpha was done. The results are indicated in Table 4.14, and was used to determine the reliability of the data.

Table 4.14
Reliability Testing

Variables	Cronbach's Alpha	No of Items
Quantitative Demand	0.862	4
Emotional Demand	0.900	3
Social Support from a Co-worker	0.720	3
Lack of Social Support from Supervisor	0.777	3
Abusive Supervision	0.975	5
Job Insecurity	0.930	3
Lack of Reward and Recognition	0.889	4
Work family Conflicts	0.968	4
Customer Incivility	0.961	5
Emotional Exhaustion	0.993	7
Mental Exhaustion	0.976	7
Physical Exhaustion	0.970	7
Turnover Intention	0.859	6

Note: Computed from Primary Data

4.6 Structural Equation Modelling

Structural Equation Modelling (SEM) is used to investigate structural relationships between variables and it is a multivariate statistical analysis technique. It is possible to investigate the structural relationship between measurable variables and latent constructs using this technique, which is a combination of component analysis and multiple regression analysis. Because it puts the proposed informal linkages to the test. The term "casual modelling" refers to the application of structural equation modelling to a situation.

Due to its ability to assign relationships between unobserved (latent) components and observed variables, structural equation modelling is widely used in the social sciences. It is possible to divide the Structural Equation Modelling process into two phases.

a) Measurement Model - Confirmatory Factor Analysis

It demonstrates how much the unseen variables contribute to the latent variable, which helps to corroborate the hypothesised factor structure pattern. The measurement model's key benefit is that it assists us in determining the measuring instrument's reliability and validity.

b) Structural Equation Model

The structural model determines the constructs independent and dependent relationships and tests the hypothesis by fitting the sample data into the model, providing the theoretical foundation of the research. As a result of using a variety of fitness indicators, this test is critical because it determines the degree to which the data in the theoretical model is fit to the model.

4.7Assessment of the Measuring Model

4.7.1 Confirmatory Factor Analysis

SEM (Structural Equation Modelling) is a confirmatory approach that provides a thorough means of validating a measurement model for latent constructs. Confirmatory Factor Analysis is a technique for verifying the data that was collected (CFA). For each latent construct involved in the investigation, the researcher must conduct CFA before modelling their interrelationship in a structural model.

Confirmatory Factor Analysis is a multivariate statistical method for evaluating if the measured variables accurately reflect the number of constructs. For ensuring data consistency in constructs, Confirmatory Factor Analysis is the most commonly used method of analysis. Confirmatory factor analysis (CFA) has become increasingly important in a variety of social and behavioural sciences fields. When used in conjunction with theory-derived models, it is a subset of the structural equation modelling technique that investigates causal relationships between latent and observable variables (Byrne, 2013). An item's fit into a specific, theory-based measurement model (in which items only load on the attributes they are designed to measure) can be determined using CFA, and potential item flaws can be identified using this method as well. Statistical model conceptualisation, identification, and parameter estimation are all part of the CFA process, which also includes data-model fit assessment and model modification.

The factor loadings on the corresponding factors of measurement items with good measurement properties should be greater than 0.45 on the corresponding factors in a CFA. If an item has a factor loading of less than 0.45, it is considered incompatible and is removed from consideration (Comrey, 1973). Alternatively, the confirmatory model is referred to as the measurement model. For this study (*Effect of Psychosocial Work Environment on Job Burnout and Turnover Intention among Retail Textile Shop Salespersons in Kerala*), the following constructs are included in the measurement model:

1. Psychosocial Work Environment
2. Job Burnout
3. Turnover Intention

4.8 Steps in Assessing the Measuring Model

To reduce the risk of misspecification, it is vital to assess the validity and reliability tests before assessing the fit indices of the proposed conceptual model (Field, 2013).

4.8.1 Validity

In layman's terms, the validity of an instrument is determined by how well it measures what it is intended to measure. (Frankfurt & Nachmias, 1996). Validity is checked to apply them in a substantial analysis. Validity refers to capacity of the instrument to measure what it claims to assess for a latent construct. Each measuring model must have three levels of validity.

4.8.2 Convergent Validity

When all of the items in a measuring model are statistically significant, the validity of the model is convergent. Computing the Average Variance Extracted for each construct could also be used to determine whether or not the constructs are convergent. It is necessary that the AVE value be at least 0.5 in order to achieve this validity (Janssens et al.,2009).

4.8.3 Construct Validity

A construct's validity is determined when the fitness indexes for that construct reach a certain level of significance. It is expressed in per cent as fitness indexes, which indicate how well the items measure the latent constructs they are intended to measure. Another method of determining the validity of the construct that effectively tests what it is intended to test. Convergent validity and discriminant validity are both considered construct validity subcategories or subtypes, and they are both considered construct validity subtypes.

4.8.4 Discriminant Validity

This validity shows that if a construct's measurement model lacks redundant components. The presence of a high Model Indices value suggests that the items in question are redundant (Hair et al., 2006). The researcher could run the measurement model without one of the identified items. The redundant pair could be constrained as the researcher's "free parameter estimate" alternatively. In addition, the correlation between exogenous constructs should not be greater than 0.85 in order for discriminant validity to be established. When the correlation between the two exogenous constructs is greater than 0.85, the two exogenous constructs are either redundant or have a significant multicollinearity issue.

4.8.5 Reliability

Reliability means the extent to which the specified measurement model is dependable in measuring the intended latent construct.

4.8.6 Composite Reliability

Composite reliability is a measure of the overall dependability of a construct. The value can be anywhere between 0 and 1. Values of composite reliability of 0.6 and higher are considered satisfactory. Values less than 0.6 indicate a lack of consistency within the system.

4.9 Fitness of a Measurement Model

According to the data set's correlation between variables, model fit refers to how well a proposed model explains fitness when applied to the data set. After taking into consideration the statistically significant correlations between the variables in the data set, the fitness is determined. If this is not the case, there is a significant 'discrepancy' between the proposed and observed correlations, resulting in a poor fit for the proposed model. In order to determine the goodness of fit, there are specific measures to use. Using the goodness of fit test, you can determine whether the 'distance' between the data input and the dispersion is within acceptable limits. If the distance between the two points is less than the threshold value, the fit is considered good (called the critical value). The values for the following thresholds have been calculated based on the information provided. Model fit can be classified into three types: absolute fit, incremental fit, and parsimonious fit.

Table 4.15
Model Fit Indices and Level of Acceptance

Name of the Category	Index	Index Full Name	Acceptance Level
Absolute Fit	Chi-square	Discrepancy Ch- square	p-value >0.05
	RMSEA	Root Mean Square of Error Approximation	RMSEA<0.08
	GFI	Goodness of Fit Index	GFI > 0.90
Incremental Fit	AGFI	Adjusted Goodness of Fit	AGFI>0.09
	CFI	Comparative Fit Index	CFI > 0.09
	TLI	Tucker-Lewis Index	TLI > 0.90
	NFI	Normed Fit Index	NFI > 0.09
Parsimonious Fit	Chisq/df	Chi Square/ Degrees of Freedom	Chisq/df < 3.0

4.9.1 Chi-square Test (χ^2 Test)

The chi-square goodness of fit indicator determines if theoretical specifications and empirical data agree. The chi-square test indicates the difference between the observed and expected covariance matrices. The only statistical test of residuals in the matrix of SEM is the Chi-square goodness of fit test. The estimate method minimises the differences between the covariance matrix and the SEM estimation covariance matrix by generating parameter values. Closer chi-square values suggest a better match, indicating that the discrepancy between the predicted and actual covariance is minimal.

4.9.2 Root Mean Square Error of Approximation - RMSEA

The difference between the observed covariance matrix per degree of freedom and the hypothesised covariance matrix, which defines the model, is measured by the RMSEA index (Chen, 2007). The RMSEA is an absolute fit index to measure how well two variables fit together.

4.9.3 Goodness of Fit Index – GFI

The Goodness of Fit Index (GFI) was an alternative to the chi-square test and was one of the first two absolute fit indices that quantified the percentage of variance. The estimated population covariance was used to calculate the proportion of variance that was accounted for. This statistic runs from 0 to 1, with values greater than 0.90 indicating a good fit.

4.9.4 Adjusted Goodness of Fit Index - AGFI

The two absolute fit indices with GFI were AGFI and AGFI, which measured the percentage of variance and were corrected for the number of parameters. AGFI, which was related to GFI, altered the GFI based on the degrees of freedom.

4.9.5 Comparative Fit Index – CFI

The Comparative Fit Index examines model fit by highlighting inconsistencies between data and the hypothesised model. Values for the comparative fit index can vary from 0 to 1, with bigger values indicating a better fit. A confirmative fit index of 0.90 or higher is appropriate for model fit.

4.9.6 Tucker – Lewis Index – TLI

The Tucker-Lewis Index (TLI) estimates the reduction in misfit per degree of freedom. Tucker and Lewis (1973) proposed this index in exploratory factor analysis, which was later adapted to the context of covariance structure analysis and labelled as the non-normed fit index. This index deviates from the norm in that its value might be negative or exceed 1.

4.9.7 Normed Fit Index - NFI

NFI, also known as the Bentler-Bonett Normed Fit Index, is an incremental measure of goodness of fit for a statistical model that is unaffected by the model's number of parameters/variables. The model of interest is compared to a model with totally uncorrelated variables to determine its fit (Ullman JB, 1996).

4.9.8 Degrees of Freedom

The degrees of freedom denote the statistical data used to estimate model parameters. The size of the covariance matrix depends on the number of indicators in the model, and determines the degree of freedom in SEM.

4.9.9. Akaike's Information Criteria (AIC)

A metric developed by the Japanese Statistician, Hirotugu Akaike, 1970. The basic idea of AIC is to penalize the inclusion of additional variables to a model. It adds a penalty that increases the error when including additional terms. The lower the AIC, the better the model.

4.9.10. **Bayesian Information Criteria (BIC)** is a variant of AIC with a stronger penalty for including additional variables to the model.

4.10 Comparison of Different Measurement Model

Table 4.16
Results for Measurement Model Comparison

CFA - Model	Chi-square	df	Ratio Chi-Sq./ df	RMSEA (CI)	CFI	AIC	BIC
Model 1: Base Model	0.828	1	0.828	0.003	1.000	389	1431
Model 2: Model combining Abusive Supervision and Job Insecurity	0.782	1	0.782	0.050	0.981	452	1531
Model 3: Model combining Quantitative Demand and Emotional Demand	0.803	1	0.803	0.061	0.960	421	1498
Model 4: Model combining all Emotional Exhaustion and Mental Exhaustion	0.791	1	0.791	0.010	0.921	441	1546
Model 5: Model combining all Social Support from Co-Workers and Abusive Supervision	0.819	1	0.819	0.075	0.873	562	1543
Model 6: Model combining Lack of Social Support from Supervisor and Abusive Supervision	0.75	1	0.75	0.1	0.799	684	1609

***Note*:** Computed from Primary Data

The six-factor model fits the data with $\chi^2 = 0.828$, df = 1. The goodness of fit indices for the model are as follow: CMIN/DF= 0.828, RMSEA= 0.003, CFI= 1.000, AIC= 389, BIC= 1431 (The larger differences in either AIC or BIC indicates stronger evidence for one model over the other, the lower the better). Each observed variable had significant factor loading at a 0.05 level, signifying convergent validity (Anderson and Gerbing, 1988). A series of CFA models (Table 4.16) showed that six-factor model fits data better than several alternative models. It rules out the possibility of measurement bias. It also indicates strong divergent validity among constructs.

4.11 Measuring Models of Psychosocial Work Environment

The Psychosocial Work Environment has nine variables, and each variable is tested with the hypothesis using the measurement model of CFA.

4.11.1. Quantitative Demand

Figure 4.1
Confirmatory Factor Analysis of Quantitative Demand

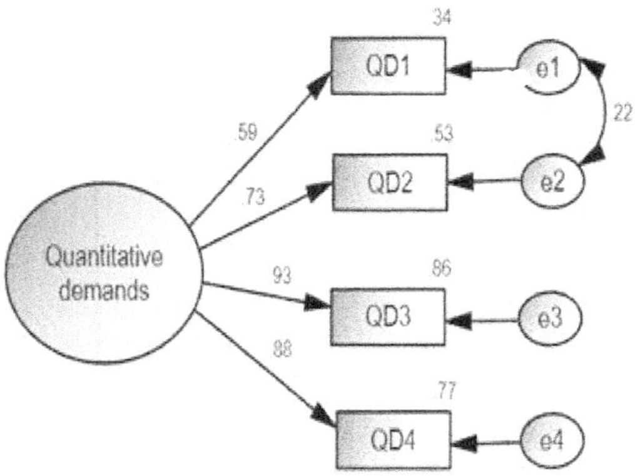

Table 4.17
Model fit Indices for CFA – Quantitative Demands

Model		DF.	Normed χ^2	GFI	AGFI	NFI	TLI	CFI	RMSEA
Quantitative demands	.828	1	.828	.999	.990	.999	1.001	1.000	.003
Recommended value	>0.05	<5	<5	>0.9	>0.9	>0.9	>0.9	>0.9	<.08

Note: Computed from Primary Data

Table 4.17 represents the CFA model fit indices to assess the overall model fit. The value of Chi-Square is. 828. Furthermore, the acceptable model's degrees of freedom ratio should be less than 5. In this case, the value is very well within the suggested maximum value. Furthermore, the RMSEA score is 0.03, well below the accepted threshold score of

0.8 (Hair et al. 2010). Moreover, the GFI and AGFI values are above 0.9, and TLI is above 0.9. Thus, the model is a good fit and can be considered for further analysis.

4.11.2. Emotional Demand

Figure 4.2
Confirmatory Factor Analysis of Emotional Demand

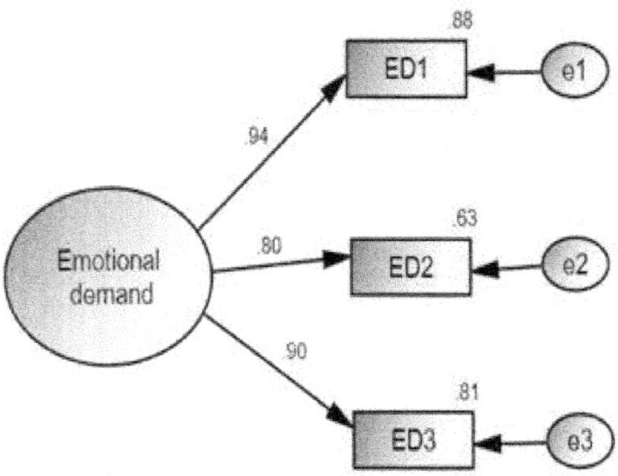

Table 4.18
Model Fit Indices for CFA – Emotional Demand

Model	χ^2	DF	Normed χ^2	GFI	AGFI	NFI	TLI	CFI	RMSEA
Emotional Demand	.070	1.388	0	1.000	.970	1.000	.981	1.000	.002
Recommended Value	>0.05	<5	<5	>0.9	>0.9	>0.9	>0.9	>0.9	<.08

Note: Computed from Primary Data

Table 4.18 represents the CFA model fit indices to assess the overall model fit. The value of Chi-Square is .070, the degrees of freedom ratio is 1.388, which is an acceptable model and less than 5. In this case, the value is very well within the suggested maximum value. Furthermore, the RMSEA score is 0.002. Moreover, the GFI is 1.000, AGFI values are above 0.970, and TLI is above 0.981. Thus, the model is a good fit and can be considered for further analysis.

4.11.3 Social Support from Co-Worker

Figure 4.3

Confirmatory Factor Analysis of Social Support from Co-Worker

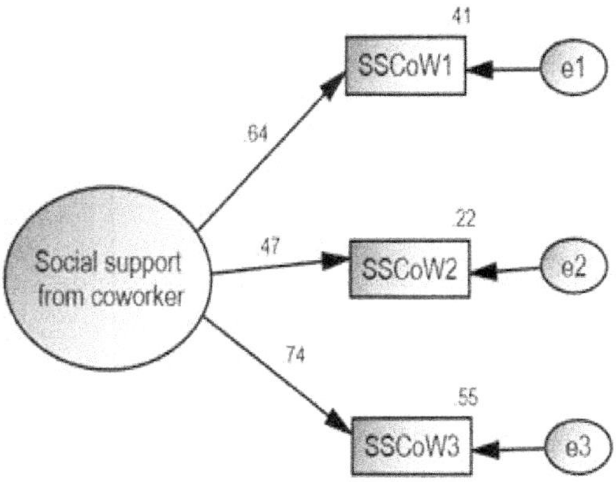

Table 4.19

Model Fit Indices for CFA – Social Support from Co-Worker

Model	χ^2	DF	Normed $\chi2$	GFI	AGFI	NFI	TLI	CFI	RMSEA
Social Support from Co-Worker	.060	1.388	0	1.000	0.910	0.947	.000	1.020	.02
Recommended Value	>0.05	<5	<5	>0.9	>0.9	>0.9	>0.9	>0.9	<.08

***Note*:** Computed from Primary Data

Table 4.19 represents the CFA model fit indices to assess the overall model fit. The value of Chi-Square is.020, degrees of freedom ratio is 1.388, which is an acceptable model and less than 5. In this case, the value is very well within the suggested maximum value. Furthermore, the RMSEA score is 0.02. Moreover, the GFI is 1.000, AGFI values are above 0.910, and TLI is above 0.947. Thus, the model is a good fit and can be considered for further analysis.

4.11.4 Lack of Social Support from Supervisor

Figure 4.4
Confirmatory Factor Analysis of Lack of Social Support from Supervisor

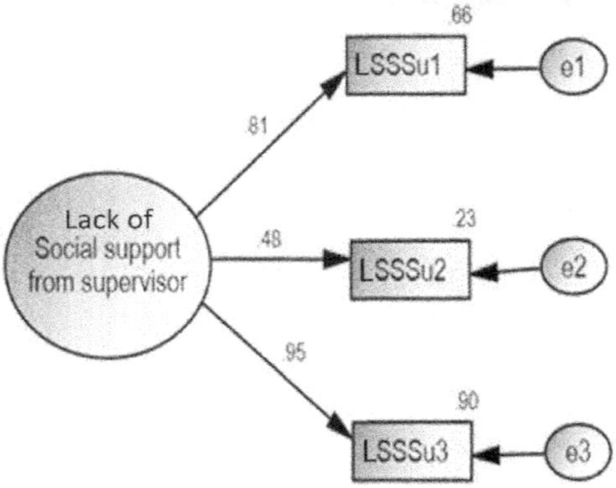

Table 4.20

Model fit Indices for CFA – Lack of Social Support from Supervisor

Model	χ^2	DF	Normed χ^2	GFI	AGFI	NFI	TLI	CFI	RMSEA
Lack of Social support from Supervisor	0.067	2.12	0	1.000	0.941	1.000	.946	1.000	.0616
Recommended Value	>0.05	<5	<5	>0.9	>0.9	>0.9	>0.9	>0.9	<.08

***Note*:** Computed from Primary Data

Table 4.20 represents the CFA model fit indices to assess the overall model fit. The value of Chi-Square is 0.067, degrees of freedom ratio is 2.12, which is an acceptable model and less than 5. In this case, the value is very well within the suggested maximum value. Furthermore, the RMSEA score is 0.0616. Moreover, the GFI is 1.000, AGFI values are above 0.910, and TLI is above 0.90. Thus, the model is a good fit and can be considered for further analysis.

4.11.5 Abusive Supervision

Figure 4.5

Confirmatory Factor Analysis of Abusive Supervision

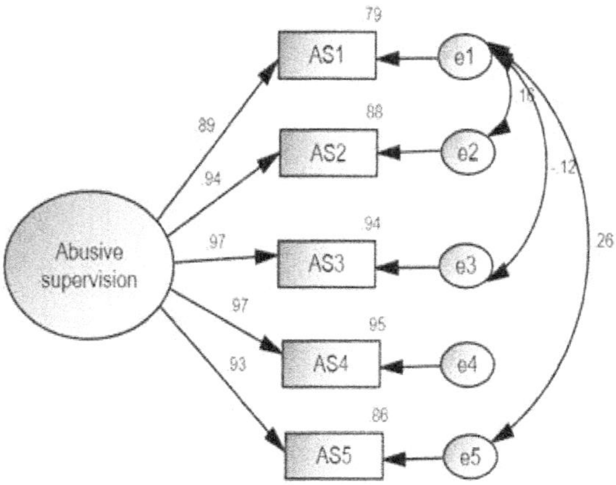

Table 4.21

Model fit Indices for CFA – Abusive Supervision

Model	χ^2	DF	Normed χ^2	GFI	AGFI	NFI	TLI	CFI	RMSEA
Abusive Supervision	3.465	2	1.733	.996	.973	.999	.998	1.000	.043
Recommended Value	>0.05	<5	<5	>0.9	>0.9	>0.9	>0.9	>0.9	<.08

Note: Computed from Primary Data

Table 4.21 shows the CFA model fit indices that can be used to evaluate the overall model fit. The Chi-Square value is 3.465, and the degrees of freedom ratio is 2, which is an acceptable model with a degree of freedom ratio less than 5. In this particular instance, the value falls well within the range of the suggested maximum value. The RMSEA score is also 0.061, which is very good. Furthermore, the GFI is 1.000, the AGFI values are greater than 0.973, and the TLI is greater than 1.101. The model thus provides a good fit and can be considered for further investigation.

4.11.6 Job insecurity

Figure 4.6
Confirmatory Factor Analysis of Job Insecurity

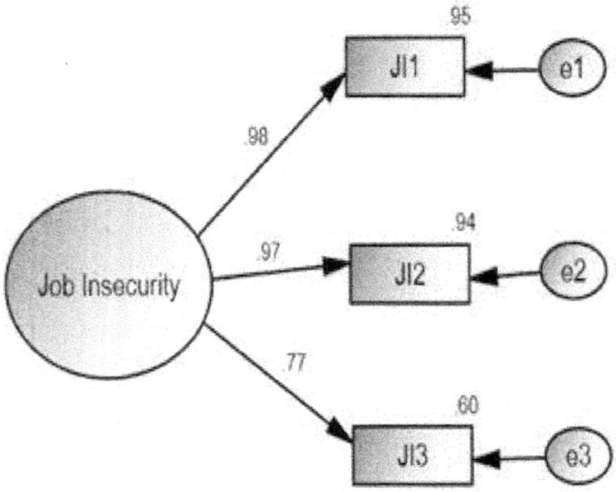

Table 4.22
Model fit Indices for CFA – Job Insecurity

Model	χ^2	DF	Normed χ^2	GFI	AGFI	NFI	TLI	CFI	RMSEA
Job Insecurity	0.059	1.6	0	1.000	.910	1.000	1.120	1.000	.036
Recommended Value	>0.05	<5	<5	>0.9	>0.9	>0.9	>0.9	>0.9	<.08

***Note*:** Computed from Primary Data

The latent constructs were significantly influenced by all of the attributes. The value of the fit indices indicates that the measurement model and the data are reasonably well matched. Table 4.22 shows that the Chi-Square value is 0.059 and that the degrees of freedom ratio is 1.6, indicating that it is an acceptable model with a degree of freedom ratio less than 5. In this particular instance, the value falls well within the range of the suggested maximum value. The RMSEA score is also 0.036, which is excellent. Furthermore, the GFI is 1.000, the AGFI values are greater than 0.910, and the TLI is 1.120. The model thus provides a good fit and can be considered for further investigation.

4.11.7 Lack of Reward and Recognition

Figure 4.7

Confirmatory Factor Analysis of Lack of Reward and Recognition

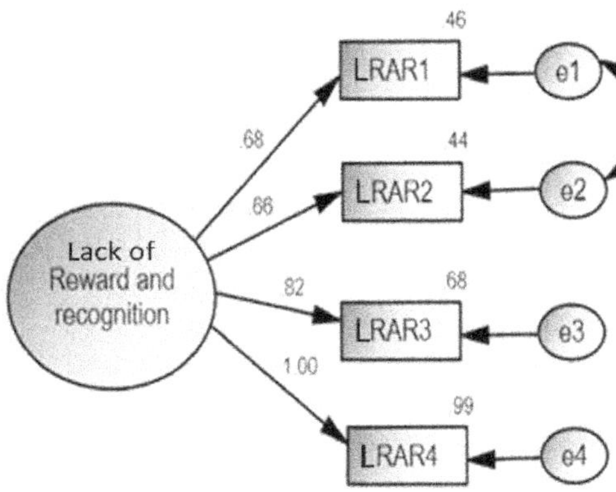

Table 4.23
Model Fit Indices for CFA – Lack of Reward and Recognition

Model	χ^2	DF	Normed χ^2	GFI	AGFI	NFI	TLI	CFI	RMSEA
Lack of Reward and recognition	0.264	2	6.632	.984	.919	.987	.968	.989	.019
Recommended Value	>0.05	<5	<5	>0.9	>0.9	>0.9	>0.9	>0.9	<.08

Note: Computed from Primary Data

The latent constructs were significantly influenced by all of the attributes. The value of the fit indices indicates that the measurement model and the data are reasonably well matched. Table 4.23 shows the CFA model fit indices that can be used to evaluate the overall model fit. The Chi-Square value is 0.264, and the degrees of freedom ratio is 2, which is an acceptable model with a degree of freedom ratio less than 5. In this particular instance, the value falls well within the range of the suggested maximum value. The RMSEA score is also 0.19, which is very good. Furthermore, the GFI value is.984, the AGFI value is.919, and the TLI value is 968. The model thus provides a good fit and can be considered for further investigation.

4.11.8 Work-Family Conflict

Figure 4.8
Confirmatory Factor Analysis of Work-Family Conflict

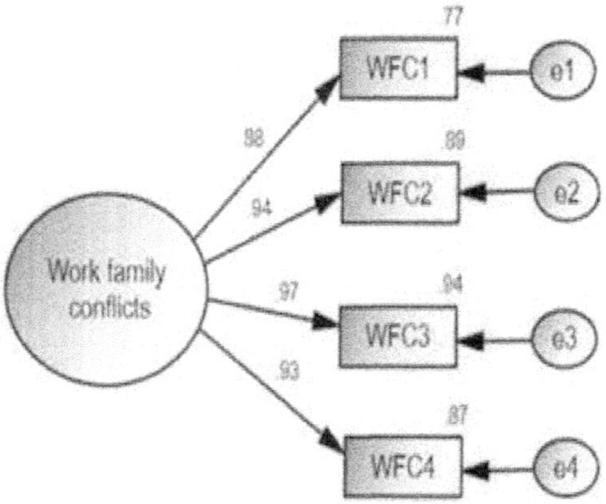

Table 4.24
Model Fit Indices for CFA – Work-Family Conflicts

Model	χ^2	DF	Normed χ^2	GFI	AGFI	NFI	TLI	CFI	RMSEA
Work family conflicts	.060	3	0	1.000	.919	1.000	.964	1.000	.094
Recommended Value	>0.05	<5	<5	>0.9	>0.9	>0.9	>0.9	>0.9	<.08

***Note*:** Computed from Primary Data

The latent constructs were significantly influenced by all of the attributes. The value of the fit indices indicates that the measurement model and the data are reasonably well matched. Table 24 shows the CFA model fit indices that can be used to evaluate the overall model fit. The Chi-Square value is 0.060, and the degrees of freedom ratio is 3, which is an acceptable model with a degree of freedom ratio less than 5. In this particular instance, the value falls well within the range of the suggested maximum value. The RMSEA score is also 0.094, which is excellent. Furthermore, the GFI value is 1.000, the AGFI value is.919, and the TLI value is 964. So, the model is a good fit and should be taken into consideration further.

4.11.9 Customer Incivility

Figure 4.9
Confirmatory Factor Analysis of Customer Incivility

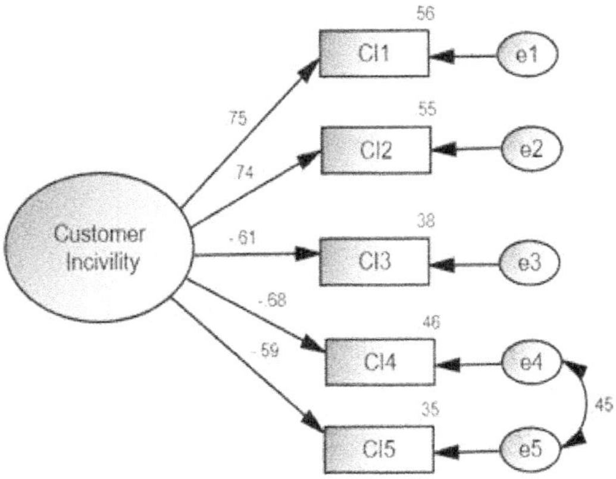

Table 4.25
Model Fit Indices for CFA- Customer Incivility

Model	χ^2	DF	Normed χ^2	GFI	AGFI	NFI	TLI	CFI	RMSEA
Customer Incivility	2.418	4	.604	.998	.991	.997	1.006	1.000	.050
Recommended Value	>0.05	<5	<5	>0.9	>0.9	>0.9	>0.9	>0.9	<.08

Note: Computed from Primary Data

The latent constructs were significantly influenced by all of the attributes. The value of the fit indices indicates that the measurement model and the data are reasonably well-matched. Table 4.25 shows the CFA model fit indices that can be used to evaluate the overall model fit. It has a value of 2.418, and the degrees of freedom ratio is 4, making it an acceptable model with a value of less than 5. In this particular instance, the value falls well within the range of the suggested maximum value. The RMSEA score is also 0.050, which is excellent. Furthermore, the GFI value is.989, the AGFI value is.991, and the TLI value is 1. 006. The model thus provides a good fit and can be considered for further investigation.

4.11.10 Assessment of Measurement Models for Item Loading and Reliability – Psychosocial Work Environment

The Psychosocial Work Environment measurement model, or CFA, is depicted in Figure 4.10 The basic goal of the CFA analysis is to see if the item's factor loadings under each dimension are more than 0.40. (Which is considered as moderate correlation value). Therefore, the factor loadings of items with a factor less than 0.40 are excluded from the SEM analysis. Table 4.26 shows the standardised loading values.

Figure 4.10

CFA for Psychosocial Work Environment

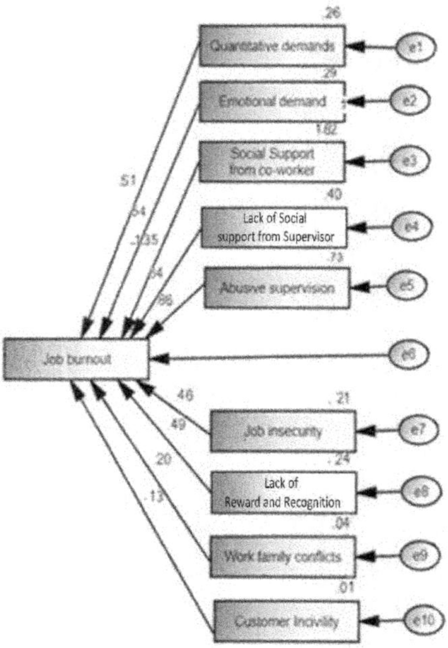

With this in mind, Table 4.26 shows the Goodness-of-Fit & Incremental Indices of Measurement model for Psychosocial Work Environment.

Table 4.26
Model fit Indices for CFA –Psychosocial Work Environment

	χ^2	DF	Normed $\chi 2$	GFI	AGFI	NFI	TLI	CFI	RMSEA
Psychosocial work environment	23.593	19	1.242	.987	.969	.996	.998	.999	.025
Recommended Value	>0.05	<5	<5	>0.9	>0.9	>0.9	>0.9	>0.9	<.08

Note: Computed from Primary Data

The Psychosocial Work Environment Goodness-of-Fit of Measurement model is depicted in Table 4.26. The Chi-square/df (2/df) (23.598), the Goodness of Fit index (0.987), the Adjusted Goodness of Fit Index (0.969), the Normed Fit Index (1.242), and the Comparative Fit Index (.999) are all well within the acceptable range, according to the results. However, the RMSEA is 0.025, far below the 0.08 suggested limit. Therefore, the model is an overidentified model with an overall acceptable fit. As a result, SEM analysis can be performed on it.

Table 4.27
Reliability and Item Loading

Constructs	Factors	Factor loading	Composite Reliability	AVE	Cronbach's Alpha
Quantitative Demand	QD1	0.742	0.840	0.566	0.817
	QD2	0.801			
	QD3	0.726			
	QD4	0.839			
Emotional Demand	ED1	0.845	0.900	0.710	0.784
	ED2	0.839			
	ED3	0.844			
Social Support from Co-worker	SsCoW1	0.841	0.897	0.719	0.872
	SsCoW2	0.882			
	SsCoW3	0.821			
Lack of Social Support	LSsSu1	0.731	0.894	0.553	0.837

from Supervisor	LSsSu2	0.763			
	LSsSu3	0.737			
Abusive Supervision	AS1	0.772	0.862	0.558	0.857
	AS2	0.732			
	AS3	0.769			
	AS4	0.769			
	AS5	0.719			
Job Insecurity	JI1	0.865	0.899	0.733	0.707
	JI2	0.875			
	JI3	0.826			
Lack of Reward and Recognition	LReRe1	0.736	0.840	0.632	0.877
	LReRe2	0.794			
	LReRe3	0.804			
	LReRe4	0.844			
Work-family conflicts	WFC1	0.878	0.841	0.729	0.846
	WFC2	0.836			
	WFC3	0.873			
	WFC4	0.828			
Customer Incivility	CI1	0.753	0.856	0.623	0.842
	CI2	0.731			
	CI3	0.793			
	CI4	0.875			
	CI5	0.788			

***Note*:** Computed from Primary Data

Note: Abbreviations- QD= Quantitative Demand; ED= Emotional Demand; SsCoW= Social Support from Co-worker; LSsSu= Lack of Social Support from Supervisor; AS= Abusive Supervision; JI= Job Insecurity; LReRe= Lack of Reward and Recognition; WFC= Work Family Conflict; CI= Customer Incivility

The CFA analysis revealed that all items had threshold values greater than 0.40, indicating convergent validity. The measuring model or CFA for Psychosocial Work Environment dimensions is depicted in Figure 4.10. The fundamental goal of the CFA analysis is to determine whether the item factor loadings under each dimension are greater than 0.40. (Which is considered as moderate correlation value). The items with factor loadings less than 0.40 are excluded from the SEM analysis. The values of composite reliability are higher than 0.6 and are considered satisfactory. The AVE values are more than 0.5, indicating convergent validity. Finally, all the variables have Cronbach alpha values above 0.7.

Table 4.28

Discriminant Validity Result for Psychosocial Work Environment

	QD	ED	SsCoW	LSsSu	AS	JI	LReRe	WFC	CI
QD	**(0.752)** *								
ED	0.654	**(0.842)***							
SsCow	0.584	0.784	**(0.847)***						
LSsSu	0.644	0.784	0.784	**(0.743)***					
AS	0.547	0.687	0.745	0.655	**(0.746)***				
JI	0.654	0.567	0.654	0.687	0.658	**(0.856)***			
LReRe	0.679	0.781	0.687	0.574	0.697	0.789	**(0.789)***		
WFC	0.687	0.674	0.547	0.564	0.578	0.745	0.647	**(0.853)***	
CI	0.541	0.684	0.539	0.621	0.678	0.687	0.678	0.749	**(0.789)***

Note: Abbreviations- QD= Quantitative Demand; ED= Emotional Demand; SsCoW= Social Support from Co-worker; LSsSu= Lack of Social Support from Supervisor; AS= Abusive Supervision; JI= Job Insecurity; LReRe= Lack of Reward and Recognition; WFC= Work Family Conflict; CI= Customer Incivility

The square roots of AVE for all constructs are bigger than the inter-item correlations for any two latent variables, as seen in Table 4.28 Therefore, they do not statistically overlap and do not have the multicollinearity problem. As a result, discriminant validity is validated (Fornell-Larcker, 1981). Since the findings of the reliability and validity tests are ideal, the SEM study of the Psychosocial Work Environment can be done. The result verifies the measurement scale's internal consistency and dependability.

4.12 The Model for Measuring Job Burnout

Job Burnout has three variables, and each variable is tested with the hypothesis using the measurement model of CFA.

4.12.1 Emotional Exhaustion

Figure 4.11
Confirmatory Factor Analysis of Emotional Exhaustion

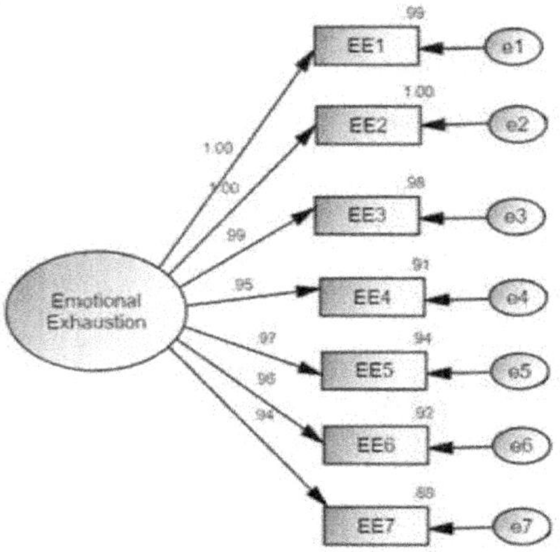

Table 4.29
Model fit Indices for CFA – Emotional Exhaustion

	χ^2	DF	Normed χ^2	GFI	AGFI	NFI	TLI	CFI	RMSEA
Emotional Exhaustion	12.25	3	3.063	.978	.847	.996	.981	.996	.033
Recommended Value	>0.05	<5	<5	>0.9	>0.9	>0.9	>0.9	>0.9	<.08

***Note*:** Computed from Primary Data

The CFA model fit indices are shown in Table 4.28 to assess the overall model fit. The Chi-Square value is 12.25, and an acceptable model should have a degree of freedom ratio of fewer than 5. The value in this Table 4.29 is 3, which is within the recommended maximum value. The RMSEA score is 0.033, significantly lower than the acceptable level. Furthermore, the GFI and AGFI values are close to 0.9, while the CFI is above 0.9, indicating an exact fit. As a result, the model fits well and may be used for future investigation.

4.12.2 Mental Exhaustion

The variable Mental Exhaustion is measured using seven items. The path diagram of the CFA model for Mental Exhaustion is shown in Figure 4.12 All the items in the model have standardised factor loading above 0.5 (Hair et al., 2010), indicating that the model is valid.

Figure 4.12

Confirmatory Factor Analysis of Mental Exhaustion

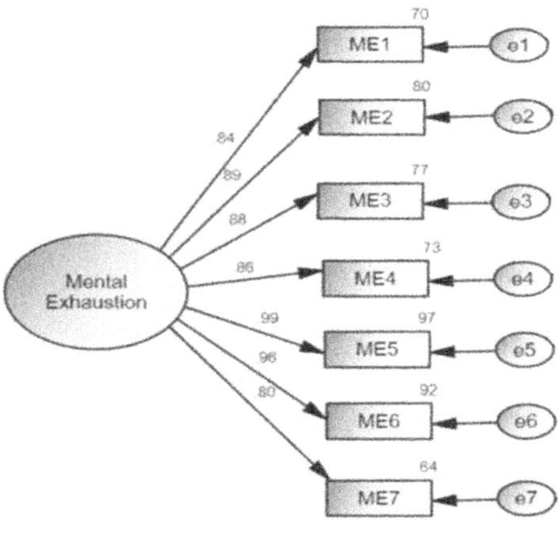

Table 4.30
Model fit Indices for CFA – Mental Exhaustion

	χ^2	DF	Normed χ^2	GFI	AGFI	NFI	TLI	CFI	RMSEA
Mental Exhaustion	1.922	6	.320	.999	.994	1.00	1.003	1.000	.000
Recommended Value	>0.05	<5	<5	>0.9	>0.9	>0.9	>0.9	>0.9	<.08

***Note*:** Computed from Primary Data

Goodness of Fit measurements of the CFA model for Mental Exhaustion is presented in Table 4.30. The values for the model fit indices show a good fit. Hence the CFA model for Mental Exhaustion was accepted.

4.12.3 Physical Exhaustion

The variable Physical Exhaustion is measured using seven items. The path diagram of the CFA model for effort is shown in Figure 4.13. All the items in the model have standardised factor loading above 0.5 (Hair et al., 2010), indicating that the model is valid.

Figure 4.13

Confirmatory Factor Analysis of Physical Exhaustion

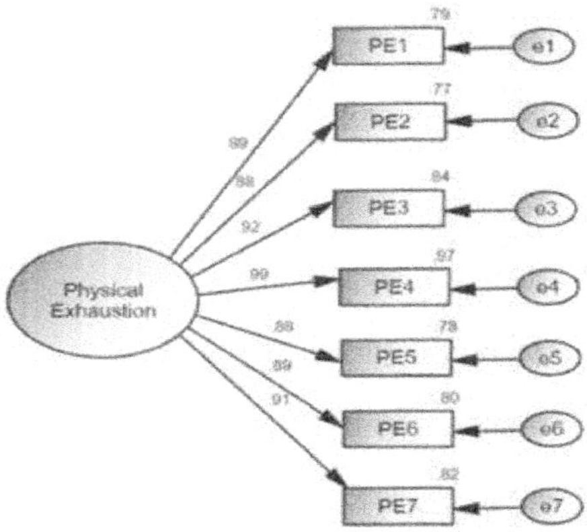

Table 4.31

Model fit Indices for CFA – Physical Exhaustion

	χ^2	DF	Normed χ^2	GFI	AGFI	NFI	TLI	CFI	RMSEA
Physical Exhaustion	8.706	7	1.244	.994	.975	.998	.999	1.000	.025
Recommended Value	>0.05	<5	<5	>0.9	>0.9	>0.9	>0.9	>0.9	<.08

***Note*:** Computed from Primary Data

Table 4.31 shows the CFA model for Physical Exhaustion's Goodness of Fit measures. Again, the model fit indices have good values, indicating a strong fit. As a result, the CFA model for the physical exhaustion was approved.

4.12.4 Assessment of Measurement Models for Item Loading and Reliability – Job Burnout

The Job Burnout model, or CFA, is depicted in Figure 4.14. The primary goal of the CFA analysis is to see if the item's factor loadings under each dimension are more than 0.40. (which is considered as moderate correlation value). Therefore, the factor loadings of items with factor loadings less than 0.40 are excluded from the SEM analysis.

Figure 4.14
CFA Analysis of Job Burnout

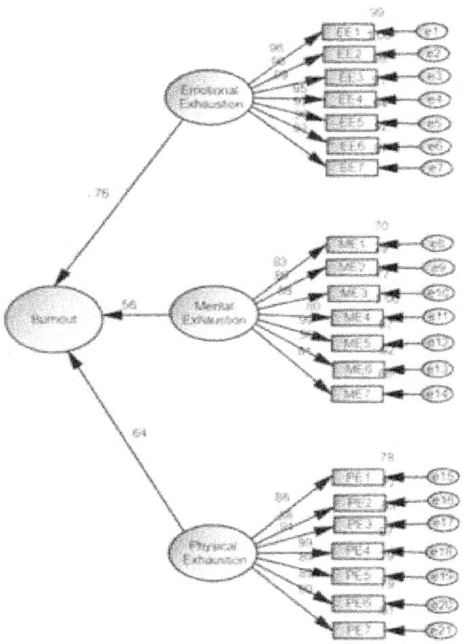

Table 4.32
Model fit Indices for CFA – Job Burnout

	χ^2	DF	Normed χ^2	GFI	AGFI	NFI	TLI	CFI	RMSEA
Job Burnout	4.398	141	3.258	.961	.609	.875	.823	.881	.071
Recommended Value	>0.05	<5	<5	>0.9	>0.9	>0.9	>0.9	>0.9	<.08

***Note*:** Computed from Primary Data

The Goodness-of-Fit measurement for Job Burnout is shown in Table 4.32. According to the results, Chi-square/df (2/df) is 4.398, within the allowed range. The Goodness of Fit index is 0.961, slightly higher than the cut-off point. The Adjusted Goodness of Fit Index (0.609) is satisfactory. The Normed Fit Index (NFI) and Comparative Fit Index (CFI) are both somewhat below the 0.90 thresholds that are suggested. The RMSEA is 0.071, which is substantially below the 0.08 suggested limit. As a result, SEM analysis is possible. Table 4.32 shows the standardised loading values.

Table 4.33
Reliability and Item Loading of Job Burnout

Constructs	Factors	Factor loading	Composite Reliability	AVE	Cronbach's Alpha
Emotional Exhaustion	EE1	0.996	0.848	0.923	0.876
	EE2	0.989			
	EE3	0.952			
	EE4	0.968			
	EE5	0.961			
	EE6	0.935			
	EE7	0.924			
Mental Exhaustion	ME1	0.835	0.811	0.858	0.787
	ME2	0.891			
	ME3	0.877			
	ME4	0.957			
	ME5	0.807			
	ME6	0.812			
	ME7	0.814			
Physical Exhaustion	PE1	0.883	0.857	0.821	0.743
	PE2	0.879			
	PE3	0.911			
	PE4	0.986			
	PE5	0.888			
	PE6	0.891			
	PE7	0.903			

Note: Abbreviations- EE= Emotional Exhaustion; ME= Mental Exhaustion; PE= Physical Exhaustion

The results demonstrate that the composite reliability scores for all constructs (dimension) are greater than 0.70 (Chin, 1998), implying that the construct is internally consistent.

4.12.5 Convergent Validity and Reliability

The loadings on most of the items in each construct are larger than 0.70, indicating convergent validity. Emotional Exhaustion has composite reliability of 0.848, Mental Exhaustion has composite reliability of 0.811, and Physical Exhaustion has composite reliability of 0.857. The results show that all constructs are more reliable than the needed level. The internal consistency of the measurements is indicated by Cronbach's alpha values of more than 0.70 across all dimensions.

4.12.6 Discriminant Validity

Table 4.34
Discriminant Validity Result for Job Burnout

	EE	ME	PE
EE	**(0.960)**		
ME	0.754	**(0.926)**	
PE	0.714	0.764	**(0.906)**

Note: Abbreviations- EE= Emotional Exhaustion; ME= Mental Exhaustion; PE= Physical Exhaustion

The square roots of AVE for all constructs are bigger than the inter-item correlations for latent variables, as seen in Table 4.34. The square root of AVE of Emotional Exhaustion is 0.960, as seen in the table. Mental Exhaustion and Emotional Exhaustion has a 0.754 intercorrelation. Mental weariness has an AVE of 0.926, and the cross-correlation between mental and physical Exhaustion is 0.764. Physical Exhaustion has an AVE of 0.906 and an inter-correlation of 0.714 between physical and emotional Exhaustion. The AVE is less than all correlation values. They do not statistically overlap and do not have the multicollinearity problem. As a result, the discriminant validity is validated (Fornell Larcker, 1981). SEM analysis of Job Burnout can be performed because the reliability and validity test results are fairly consistent.

4.13 The Model for Measuring Turnover Intention

4.13.1 Assessment of Measurement Models for Item Loading and Reliability – Turnover Intention

The turnover Intention model, or CFA, is depicted in Figure 4.15. The basic goal of the CFA analysis is to see if the item's factor loadings under each dimension are more than 0.40. (which is considered a moderate correlation value). Therefore, the factor loadings of items with factor loadings less than 0.40 are excluded from the SEM analysis. Table 4.35 shows the standardised loading values.

Figure 4.15
CFA Analysis of Turnover Intention

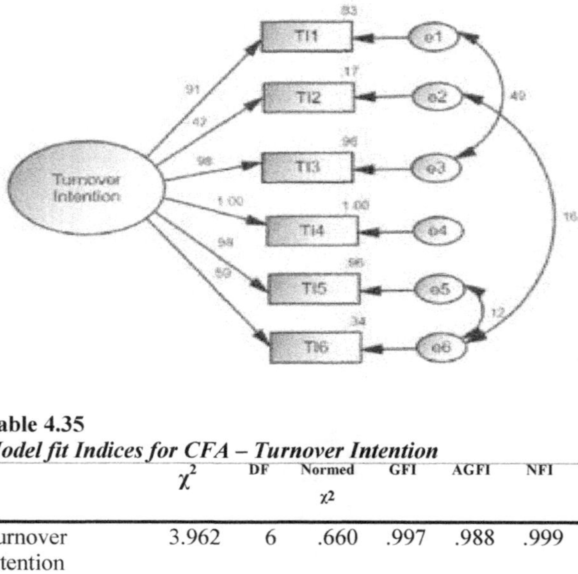

Table 4.35
Model fit Indices for CFA – Turnover Intention

	χ^2	DF	Normed χ^2	GFI	AGFI	NFI	TLI	CFI	RMSEA
Turnover Intention	3.962	6	.660	.997	.988	.999	1.001	1.000	.000
Recommended Value	>0.05	<5	<5	>0.9	>0.9	>0.9	>0.9	>0.9	<.08

Note**:** Computed from Primary Data

Table 4.35 shows the CFA model for Turnover Intention Goodness of Fit measures. Again, the model fit indices have good values, indicating a solid fit. As a result, the CFA model for the effort was approved.

Table 4.36
Reliability and Item Loading of Turnover Intention

Constructs	Factors	Factor loading	Composite Reliability	AVE	Cronbach's Alpha
Turnover Intention	TI1	0.996	0.842	0.935	0.802
	TI2	0.989			
	TI3	0.952			
	TI4	0.968			
	TI5	0.961			
	TI6	0.935			

Note: Computed from Primary Data

The results show that the composite reliability values for all the constructs are greater than 0.70, confirming the internal consistency of the construct.

4.13.2 Convergent Validity and Reliability

Each construct's loadings are more than 0.70, indicating convergent validity. The data show that Turnover Intention necessitates consistency. Because Cronbach's alpha is greater than 0.70, it shows that the metrics are internally consistent.

4.14 Structural Equation Model

In this study, the structural equation model is used to determine the independent, dependent, and mediating relationships between the Psychosocial Work Environment, Job Burnout, and Turnover Intention. The hypothesis is tested by fitting the sample data into the model, which serves as the theoretical foundation for the research findings.

4.15 Proposed Conceptual Framework

The proposed conceptual framework is shown below in figure 4.16. The proposed model illustrates the relationship between the constructs of Psychosocial Work Environment, Job Burnout and Turnover Intention.

Figure 4.16: *Conceptual frame Work Using Structural Equation Modelling*

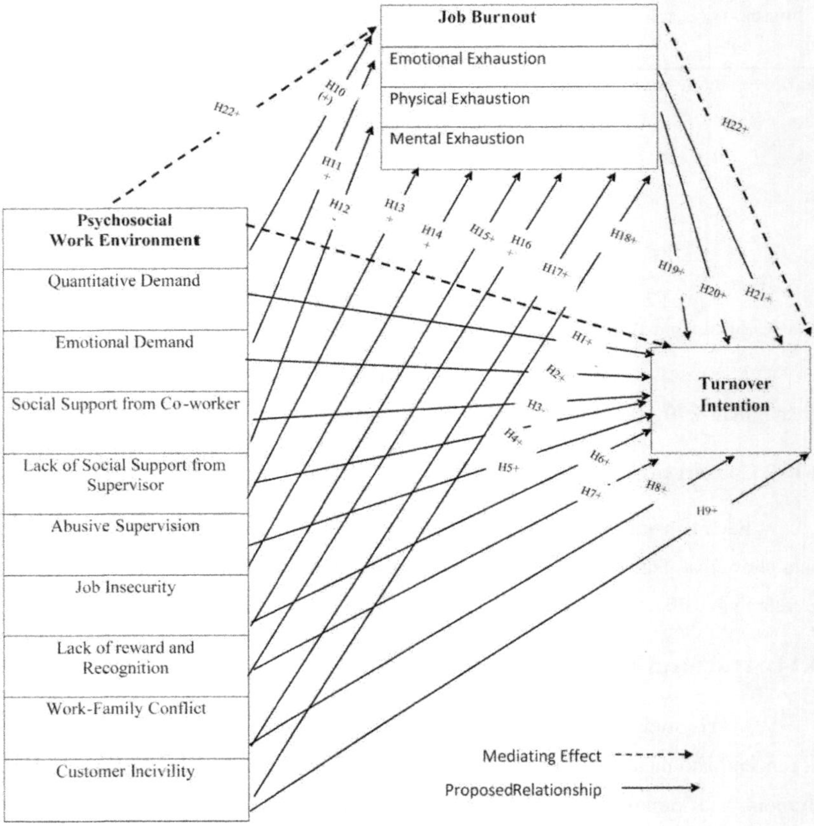

4.16 Objective 1

To study the effect of Psychosocial Work Environment on Turnover Intention

4.16.1 Research Question 1

Does the Psychosocial Work Environment affect Retail Textile Salespersons' Turnover Intention?

4.16.2 Hypotheses of the Study

The relationship between Psychosocial Work Environment and Turnover Intention is hypothesised as follows. The nine hypotheses about the relationship between Psychosocial Work Environment and Turnover Intentions are:

Table 4.37 *Hypotheses of the Study*

Hypothesis #	Objectives and Hypotheses
	Objective: To study the effect of Psychosocial Work Environment on Turnover Intention, which was studied by finding out the effect of Quantitative Demand, Emotional Demand, Social Support from Co-workers, Lack of Social Support from Supervisor, Abusive Supervision, Job Insecurity, Lack of Reward and Recognition, Work-Family Conflicts, and Customer Incivility on Turnover Intention
H_1	Quantitative Demand has positive influence on Turnover Intention
H_2	Emotional Demand has positive influence on Turnover Intention
H_3	Social Support from Co-worker has negative influence on Turnover Intention
H_4	Lack of Social Support from Supervisor has positive influence on Turnover Intention
H_5	Abusive Supervision has positive influence on Turnover Intention
H_6	Job Insecurity has positive influence on Turnover Intention
H_7	Lack of Reward and Recognition has positive influence on Turnover Intention
H_8	Work-Family Conflict has positive influence on Turnover Intention
H_9	Customer Incivility has positive influence on Turnover Intention

Figure 4.17
Effect of Psychosocial Work Environment on Turnover Intention

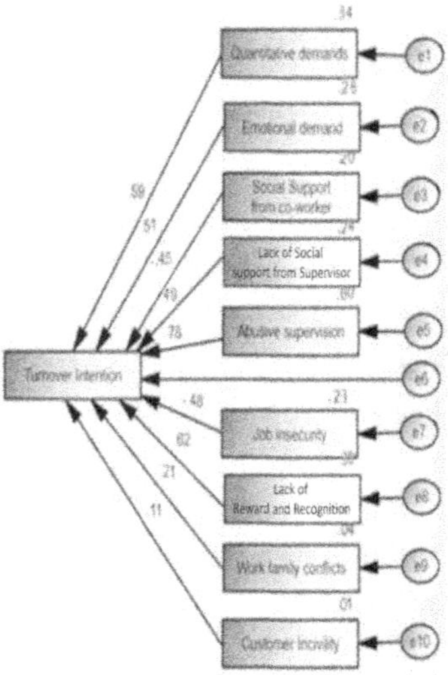

Table 4.38
Model fit Indices - Psychosocial Work-Environment - Turnover Intention

	χ^2	DF	Normed χ^2	GFI	AGFI	NFI	TLI	CFI	RMSEA
Psychosocial Work-Environment - Turnover Intention	.153	1.389	58.17	.977	.963	.977	.597	.993	.030
Recommended value	>0.05	<5	<5	>0.9	>0.9	>0.9	>0.9	>0.9	<.08

***Note*:** Computed from Primary Data

This study looked at the adjusted GFI 0.977 and RMSEA 0.030 for incremental fit metrics, as Hair et al. (1998) indicated. The AGFI (0.963), NFI (0.977), and CFI (0.993) values in the model show an intense match. GFI, AGFI, NFI, and CFI > 0.9 suggest a good match between data and model, whereas GFI > 0.85, NFI 0.9, and 0.8 AGFI 0.9 imply an acceptable model. Therefore, the proposed model is well-fitting and meets the researcher's suggested criteria. The statistic derived with the degrees of freedom yields a decent fit of 1.389, which falls within the acceptable fit range. Table 4.38 shows the standardised structural coefficients and hypotheses test findings.

Table 4.39
Standardised Structural Coefficients and Hypotheses Results; Psychosocial Work Environment and Turnover Intention

Relationship	**Estimate**	**Critical Ratio (CR)**	**p-value**	**Decision**
Quantitative Demand → Turnover Intention	0.598	13.407	<0.001***	**Significant**
Emotional Demand → Turnover Intention	0.512	8.705	<0.001***	**Significant**
Social Support from Co-worker → Turnover Intention	-.452	20.565	<0.001***	**Significant**
Lack Social Support from Supervisor → Turnover Intention	0.494	8.849	<0.001***	**Significant**
Abusive supervision → Turnover Intention	0.781	-20.827	<0.001***	**Significant**
Job Insecurity → Turnover Intention	0.481	-4.907	<0.001***	**Significant**
Lack of Reward and Recognition → Turnover Intention	0.620	14.409	<0.001***	**Significant**
Work Family Conflicts → Turnover Intention	0.216	2.934	0.038	**Not Significant**
Customer Incivility → Turnover Intention	0.107	2.135	0.033	**Not Significant**

Note: ***Significant p-Value<0.001
***Note*:** Computed from Primary Data

Table 4.39 presented Regression weights for the different predictor variables on the outcome variable. From the value of the estimate, it is clear that Abusive Supervision has the highest effect on Turnover Intention (β = 0.781). Customer Incivility (β= 0.107) and Work-Family Conflict (β=0.216) has no significant influence on Turnover Intention.

***H_1**: Quantitative Demand has positive influence on Turnover Intention*

The analysis showed that Quantitative Demand has a significant positive relationship with Turnover Intention (β=0.598). The effect of Quantitative Demand was found to be statistically significant since the p-value was <0.001. Hence *Hypothesis H_1 is Accepted.* Previous studies also found that Quantitative Demand showed a significant positive relationship between Quantitative Demand and Turnover Intention(Diana Purba et al., 2019; Jones et al., 2007)

***H**₂: Emotional Demand has positive influence on Turnover Intention*

The analysis has found that Emotional Demand has a positive and significant influence on Turnover Intention (β=0.512). The effect of Emotional Demand was found to be statistically significant since the p-value was <0.001. Hence H*ypothesis H_2 is Accepted.* This was consistent with the findings of Jones et al. (2007); Anitha & James (2016).

***H_3**: Social Support from Co-worker has negative influence on Turnover Intention*

The analysis has found that Social Support from Co-worker has a negative and significant influence on Turnover Intention (β= -.452). The effect of Social Support from Co-worker was statistically significant since the p-value was <0.001. Hence H*ypothesis H_3 is Accepted.*

According to previous studies, Social Support from Co-worker has a significant negative relationship with Turnover Intention among Co-workers is significant in shaping intentions to depart and actual turnover behaviour. Several meta-analyses found that co-worker support was negatively connected to Intention to leave (Chiaburu &Harrison,2008; Ng and Sorensen,2008; Feeley, Moon, Kozey, and Slowe, 2010).

***H_4**: Lack of Social Support from Supervisor has positive influences Turnover Intention*

According to the analysis results, lack of supervisors' social support positively influences turnover intention (β= 0.494). The effect of Lack of Social Support from the Supervisor was statistically significant since the p-value was <0.001. Hence *Hypothesis H_4 is Accepted.*

As a result of the analysis, the researcher has discovered certain undesirable features in the supervisor-salesperson relationship. Salespersons are more likely to leave the job if their supervisors do not provide social assistance. The findings of this study are consistent with those of earlier research (Cropanzano,Dasborough, & Weiss, 2017; Chen & Liu, 2019; Seo, Nahrgang, Carter, & Hom, 2018).

***H_5**: Abusive Supervision has positive influence on Turnover Intention*

Abusive Supervision is positively influencing Turnover Intention among salespersons (β= 0.781). The effect of Abusive Supervision was statistically significant since the p-value was <0.001. Hence *Hypothesis H_5 is Accepted.*

Recent studies are also supporting the result of this study. The best leaders make every effort to guarantee that their followers receive equitable treatment so that no employees feel alone or alienated from the organisation (Lyu,2018; Saleem et al.,2021).

H_6*: *Job Insecurity has positive influence on Turnover Intention

As shown in Table 4.38, Job Insecurity has a significant positive influence on Turnover Intention among salespersons (β= 0.481). The effect of Job Insecurity was found to be statistically significant since the p-value was <0.001. Hence *Hypothesis H_6 is Accepted.* The significant positive influence of Job Insecurity on Turnover Intention is consistent with findings of (Dubey, n.d; Pandey et al., 2019).

H_7*: *Lack of Reward and Recognition has positive influence on Turnover Intention

From Table 4.38, it is evident that Lack of Reward and Recognition have a significant positive influence on turnover intention among salespersons (β= 0.620). The effect of lack of Reward and Recognition was statistically significant since the p-value was <0.001. Hence *Hypothesis H_7 is Accepted.* In addition, recent study results revealed a positive relationship with turnover intention (Stahl et al., 2009; Dubey, n.d.).

H_8*: *Work-Family Conflict has positive influence on Turnover Intention

From the analysis results of the study, it is evident that Work-family support has a positive but not a significant influence on Turnover Intention among salespersons (β=0.216). The effect of Work-Family Conflict was found statistically not significant since the p-value was above <0.001. Hence *Hypothesis H_8 is Accepted.* Previous studies like Pasewark & Viator (2006); Lu et al. (2017) shows a significant positive effect on Turnover Intention.

H_9*: *Customer Incivility has positive influence on Turnover Intention

Customer Incivility has a positive but no significant influence on Turnover Intention among salespersons in retail textile shops in Kerala(β=0.107). The effect of Customer Incivility was found statistically not significant since the p-value was above <0.001. Hence *Hypothesis H_9 is Accepted.* This result does not correspond with previous studies like Chen & Wang (2019); Hans, Bonn & Cho (2016). However, most of the previous studies suggest that customer incivility significantly influences turnover intention.

Table 4.40
Summary of the Hypotheses Results

	Hypothesis Statements	Results
H_1	Quantitative demand has positive influence on Turnover Intention	**Accepted**
H_2	Emotional demand has positive influence on Turnover Intention	**Accepted**
H_3	Social Support from Co-worker has negative influence on Turnover Intention	**Accepted**
H_4	Lack of Social Support from supervisors has positive influence on Turnover Intention	**Accepted**
H_5	Abusive Supervision has positive influence on Turnover Intention	**Accepted**
H_6	Job Insecurity has positive influence on Turnover Intention	**Accepted**
H_7	Lack of Reward and Recognition has positive significant influence on Turnover Intention	**Accepted**
H_8	Work-Family conflict has positive influence on Turnover Intention	**Accepted**
H_9	Customer Incivility has positive influence on Turnover Intention	**Accepted**

4.17 Objective 2

To study the effect of Psychosocial Work Environment on Job Burnout

4.17.1 Research Question 2

Does the retail textile shop's Psychosocial Work Environment affect Salespersons' Job Burnout?

4.17.2 Hypotheses of the Study

The relationship between Psychosocial Work Environment and Job Burnout is hypothesised as follows. Nine hypotheses are formulated based on the second objective of the study.

Table 4.41
Hypotheses of the Study

Hypothesis #	Objectives and Hypothesis
Objective: To study the effect of Psychosocial Work Environment on Job Burnout, which was studied by finding out the effect of Quantitative Demand, Emotional Demand, Social Support from Co-worker, Lack of Social Support from Supervisor, Abusive Supervision, Job Insecurity, Lack of Reward and Recognition, Work-Family Conflicts, and Customer Incivility on Turnover Intention	
H_{10}	Quantitative Demand has positive influence on Job Burnout
H_{11}	Emotional Demand has positive influence on Job Burnout
H_{12}	Social Support from Co-worker has negative influence on Job Burnout
H_{13}	lack of Social Support from Supervisor has positive influence on Job Burnout
H_{14}	Abusive Supervision has positive influence on Job Burnout
H_{15}	Job Insecurity has positive influence on Job Burnout
H_{16}	Lack of Reward and Recognition has positive influence on Job Burnout
H_{17}	Work-Family Conflict has positive influence on Job Burnout
H_{18}	Customer Incivility has positive influence on Job Burnout

Figure 4.18
Effect of Psychosocial Work Environment on Job Burnout

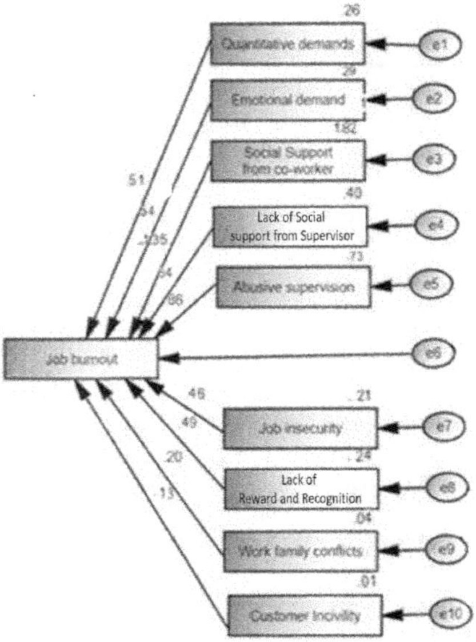

Table 4.42
Model fit Indices - Psychosocial Work-Environment – Job Burnout

	χ^2	DF	Normed χ^2	GFI	AGFI	NFI	TLI	CFI	RMSEA
Psychosocial Work-Environment - Job burnout	1.190	2	.469	.912	.603	.910	.943	.914	.336
Recommended Value	>0.05	<5	<5	>0.9	>0.9	>0.9	>0.9	>0.9	<.08

Note: Computed from Primary Data

In Table 4.42, the adjusted GFI 0.914 and RMSEA.336 for incremental fit metrics. The AGFI (0.963), NFI (0.977), and CFI (0.993) values in the model show an intense match. GFI, AGFI, NFI, and CFI > 0.9 suggest a good match between data and model, whereas GFI > 0.85, NFI 0.9, and 0.8 AGFI 0.9 imply an acceptable model. Therefore, the proposed model is well-fitting. The statistic derived with the degrees of freedom yields a decent fit of 1.190, which falls within the acceptable fit range. Table 4.42 shows the standardised structural coefficients and hypotheses test findings.

Table 4.43

Standardised Structural Coefficients and Hypotheses Results; Psychosocial Work Environment and Job Burnout

Relationship	**Estimate**	**Critical Ratio (CR)**	**p-value**	**Decision**
Quantitative Demand → Job Burnout	0.5107	4.174	<0.001***	**Significant**
Emotional Demand → Job Burnout	0.548	2.760	<0.001***	
Social Support from Co-worker → Job burnout	-1.35	2.619	<0.001***	**Significant**
Lack of Social Support from Supervisor → Job Burnout	0.543	2.862	<0.001***	**Significant**
Abusive Supervision → Job Burnout	0.863	1.254	<0.001***	**Significant**
Job Insecurity → Job Burnout	0.461	3.228	<0.001***	**Significant**
Lack of Reward and Recognition → Job Burnout	0.494	3.905	<0.001***	**Significant**
Work-Family Conflicts → Job Burnout	0.205	3.926	0.487	**Not Significant**
Customer Incivility → Job Burnout	0.134	0.676	0.499	**Not Significant**

Note: ***Significant p-Value<0.001
Note: Computed from Primary Data

From Table 4.43 presented regression weights for the different predictor variables on the outcome variable. From the value of the estimate, it is clear that Abusive Supervision has the highest effect on Job Burnout (β = 0.863). Customer Incivility (β= 0.134) and Work-Family Conflict (β=0.205) has no significant influence on Job Burnout.

***H_{10}**: Quantitative Demand has positive influence on Job Burnout*

Quantitative demand has a significant positive influence on Job Burnout (β = 0.5107). The effect of Quantitative Demand was found to be statistically significant since the p-value was <0.001. Hence *Hypothesis H_{10} is Accepted.* A previous literature review of studies in the retail sector has shown that traditional risk factors like quantitative demand positively affect Job Burnout. (Chung et al.,2017; Hwang, Kim& Rankin., 2017; Jung& Shim., 2011).

H_{11}*: *Emotional Demand has positive influence on Job Burnout

Emotional Demand has a significant positive influence on Job Burnout (β =0.548). The effect of Emotional Demand was found to be statistically significant since the p-value was <0.001. Hence *Hypothesis H_{11} is Accepted.*

This analysis result is similar to the previous studies (Jimmieson et al., 2017; Sulsky & Smith, 2005). According to Grandey (2003) and Le Blanc et al. (2001), emotional demands and Burnout have predominantly been found in service sector jobs. Bakker and Heuven(2006), in their study among nurses and studies among police officers and human service workers and care providers (Kop, Euwema, & Schaufeli, 1999), found that Emotional Demand is positively related to Job Burnout.

H_{12}*: *Social Support from Co-Worker has negative influence on Job Burnout

Social Support from Co-worker has a significant negative influence on Job Burnout (β=-1.35). The effect of Social Support from Co-Worker was statistically significant since the p-value was <0.001. Hence *Hypothesis is Accepted.* It is consistent with the findings of (Mayo et al. (2012); Sloan (2012).

H_{13}*: *Lack of Social Support from Supervisor has positive influence on Job Burnout

The study results reveal that Lack of Social Support from supervisors has a significant positive influence on Job Burnout (β=0.543). The effect of Social Support from the Supervisor was statistically significant since the p-value was <0.001. Hence *Hypothesis H_{13} is Accepted.* It is consistent with the findings of (Beehr, 1995; van den Tooren & de Jonge, 2011).

H_{14}*: *Abusive Supervision has positive influence on Job Burnout

Abusive Supervision has a significant positive effect on Job Burnout (β=0.863). The effect of Abusive Supervision was statistically significant since the p-value was <0.001. Hence *Hypothesis H_{14} is Accepted.* It is consistent with the findings of (Jiang &Gu, 2016; Gabler et al., 2014).

***H_{15}**: Job Insecurity has positive influence on Job Burnout*

The analysis result shows a significant and positive influence of Job Insecurity on Job Burnout (β= 0.461). The effect of Job Insecurity was found to be statistically significant since the p-value was <0.001. Hence *Hypothesis H_{15} is Accepted.* These results support the findings of Schaufeli & Greenglass (2001); Powell (2020).

***H_{16}**: Lack Reward and Recognition has positive influence on Job Burnout*

Lack of Reward and Recognition has a significant positive influence on Job Burnout (β= 0.494). The effect of *Lack Reward and Recognition* was statistically significant since the p-value was <0.001. Hence *Hypothesis H_{16} is Accepted.* These results support the findings of Wu et al. (2009); Bennett, Ross& Sunderland, (1996)

***H_{17}**: Work-Family conflict has positive influence on Job Burnout*

Work-Family conflict has positive influence on job burnout (β= 0.205). The effect of Work-Family Conflict was found positive but statistically not significant since the p-value was above <0.001. Hence *Hypothesis H_{17} is Accepted.* The findings are not supporting the previous studies (Ahuja et al.,2007; Alam, Sattar& Chaudhury,2011).

***H_{18}**: Customer Incivility has positive influence on Job Burnout*

Customer Incivility has a positive but no significant influence on Job Burnout among salesperson in the retail textile shops in Kerala (β=0.107). The effect of Customer Incivility was found statistically not significant since the p-value was above <0.001. Hence *Hypothesis H_{18} is Accepted.* This result is not supporting the previous results (Prasetyo et al., 2021; Hans et al., 2016).

Table 4.44
Summary of the Hypotheses Results

	Hypothesis Statements	Results
H_{10}	Quantitative Demand has positive influence on Job Burnout	**Accepted**
H_{11}	Emotional Demand has positive influence on Job Burnout	**Accepted**
H_{12}	Social Support from Co-worker has negative influence on Job Burnout	**Accepted**
H_{13}	Lack of Social Support from Supervisor has positive significant influence on Job Burnout	**Accepted**
H_{14}	Abusive Supervision has positive influence on Job Burnout	**Accepted**
H_{15}	Job Insecurity has positive influence on Job Burnout	**Accepted**
H_{16}	Lack of Reward and Recognition has positive influence on Job Burnout	**Accepted**
H_{17}	Work-Family conflict has positive influence on Job Burnout	**Accepted**
H_{18}	Customer Incivility has positive influence on Job Burnout	**Accepted**

4.18 Objective 3

To examine the effect of Job Burnout on Turnover Intention

4.18.1 Research Question 3

Does the Psychosocial Work Environment and Job Burnout have any influence on Salespersons' Turnover Intention?

4.18.2 Hypotheses of the Study

Three hypotheses are formulated based on the third objective of the study

Table 4.45
Hypotheses of the Study

Hypothesis #	Objectives and Hypotheses
Objective: To study the effect of Job Burnout on Turnover Intention, which was studied by finding out the effect of Emotional Exhaustion, Mental Exhaustion and Physical Exhaustion on Turnover Intention	
H19	Emotional Exhaustion has positive influence on Turnover Intention
H20	Mental Exhaustion has positive influence on Turnover Intention
H21	Physical Exhaustion has positive influence on Turnover Intention

Figure 4.19
Effect of Job Burnout on Turnover Intention

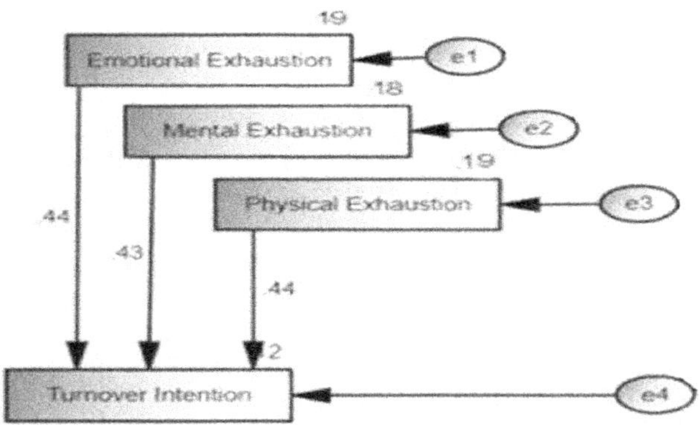

Table 4.46
Model fit Indices - Burnout - Turnover Intention

	χ^2	DF	Normed $\chi 2$	GFI	AGFI	NFI	TLI	CFI	RMSEA
Burnout - Turnover Intention	13.333	3	.435	.673	.910	.918	.976	.918	1.046
Recommended Value	>0.05	<5	<5	>0.9	>0.9	>0.9	>0.9	>0.9	<.08

***Note*:** Computed from Primary Data

In Table 4.46, the adjusted GFI 0.914 and RMSEA.336 for incremental fit metrics. The AGFI (0.963), NFI (0.977), and CFI (0.993) values in the model show an intense match. GFI, AGFI, NFI, and CFI > 0.9 suggest a good match between data and model, whereas GFI > 0.85, NFI 0.9, and 0.8 AGFI 0.9 imply an acceptable model. Therefore, the proposed model is well-fitting. The statistic derived with the degrees of freedom yields a decent fit of 1.190, which falls within the acceptable fit range. Table 4.46 shows the standardised structural coefficients and hypotheses test findings.

Table 4.47
Standardised Structural Coefficients and Hypotheses Results; Job Burnout and Turnover Intention

Relationship	Estimate	Critical Ratio (CR)	p-value	Decision
Emotional Exhaustion → Turnover Intention	0.442	9.435	0.001***	**Accepted**
Mental Exhaustion → Turnover Intention	0.434	9.238	0.001***	**Accepted**
Physical Exhaustion → Turnover Intention	0.439	9.361	0.001***	**Accepted**

Source: Primary Data

***H_{19}**: Emotional Exhaustion has positive influence on Turnover Intention*

The analysis result shows a significant and positive influence of Emotional Exhaustion on Turnover Intention (β= 0.442). The effect of Emotional Exhaustion was statistically significant since the p-value was <0.001. Hence *Hypothesis H_{19} is Accepted.* Analysis result of the current study shows that Emotional Exhaustion has a significant positive influence on Turnover Intention (Kundsen, Ducharme&Roman,2009).

***H_{20}**: Mental Exhaustion has positive influence on Turnover Intention*

The analysis result shows a significant and positive influence of Mental Exhaustion on Turnover Intention (β= 0.434). The effect of Mental Exhaustion was found to be statistically significant since the p-value was <0.001. Hence *Hypothesis H_{20} is Accepted.*

***H_{21}**: Physical Exhaustion has positive influence on Turnover Intention*

The analysis report shows that Physical Exhaustion has a significant positive influence on turnover intention (β= 0.439). The effect of Physical Exhaustion was statistically significant since the p-value was <0.001. Hence *Hypothesis H_{21} is Accepted.*

Table 4.48
Summary of the Hypotheses Results

	Hypothesis Statements	Results
H_{19}:	Emotional Exhaustion has positive influence on Turnover Intention	**Accepted**
H_{20}:	Mental Exhaustion has positive influence on Turnover Intention	**Accepted**
H_{21}:	Physical Exhaustion has positive influence on Turnover Intention	**Accepted**

4.19 Objective 4

To Examine the Mediating Effect of Job Burnout on Psychosocial Work Environment and Turnover Intention

4.19.1 Research Question 4

Is there any mediating role of job burnout on the relationship between psychosocial work environment and salespersons' turnover intentions?

4.19.2 Hypotheses of the Study

H_{22}: *Job Burnout has mediating effect on the relationship between Psychosocial Work Environment and Turnover Intention*

Mediating analysis was conducted to study the mediating effect of Job Burnout on the Psychosocial Work Environment and Turnover Intention.

4.19.3 Direct Effect of Psychosocial Work Environment on Turnover Intention

Initially, direct effect was analysed between Psychosocial Work Environment and Turnover Intention.

Figure 4.20

Direct Effect

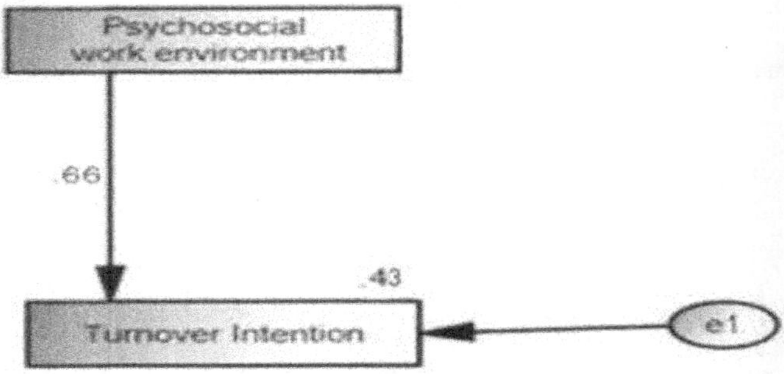

Figure 4.20 shows the direct effect of the Psychosocial Work Environment on Turnover Intention. The result of the direct effect model indicates that the path coefficient value was 0.66, and the model was significant (P< 0.001).

4.19.4 Indirect Effect of Job Burnout on Psychosocial Work environment and Turnover Intention

The indirect effect was measured by introducing the mediation variable Job Burnout. The introduction of the mediating variable (Job Burnout) has significantly impacted the relationship between the predictor variable Psychosocial Work Environment and the dependent variable Turnover Intention. However, the path coefficient between Psychosocial Work Environment and Turnover Intention has reduced from 0.66 to 0.44. Thus, the mediation analysis results indicate that "*partial mediation*" has been reported due to the mediation effect of the variable Job Burnout on the relationship between Psychosocial Work Environment and Turnover Intention.

Figure 4. 21

Mediating Effect

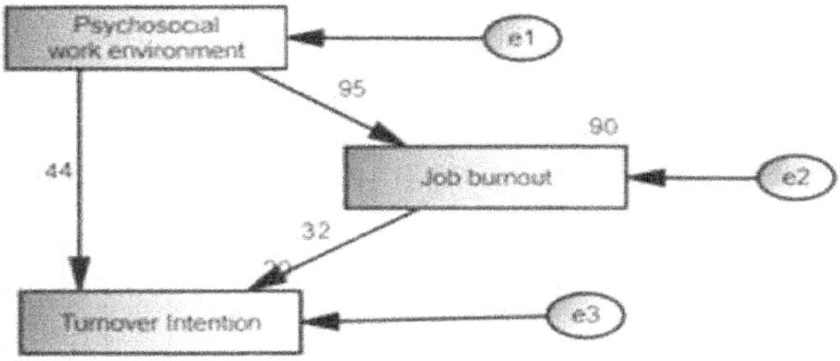

Table 4.49
Model fit Indices

Model	χ^2	D.F.	P	Normed χ^2	GFI	AGFI	NFI	TLI	CFI	RMSEA
Mediation Effect	.828	1	.363	.828	.999	.990	.999	1.001	1.000	.003
Recommended Value	>0.05	<5	>0.05	<5	>0.9	>0.9	>0.9	>0.9	>0.9	<.08

***Note*:** Computed from Primary Data

The latent constructs were significantly influenced by all of the attributes. The value of the fit indices indicates that the measurement model and the data are reasonably well matched. Following the application of the chi-square value, the DF, GFI, AGFI, NFI, TLI, CFI, and RMSEA all demonstrate a high level of model fitness.

Table 4.50
Direct and Indirect Effect of Psychosocial Work Environment, Job Burnout, and Turnover Intention.

The Regression Coefficients	Estimate	Critical Ratio (CR)	p-value
Psychosocial Work Environment → Turnover Intention (C)	0.661	9.410	<0.001
Psychosocial Work Environment → Job Burnout (A)	0.952	36.822	<0.001
Job Burnout → Turnover Intention (B)	0.232	4.696	<0.001
Psychosocial Work Environment → Turnover Intention (C')	0.221	4.466	<0.001
Mediation effect	0.440	4.445	<0.001

***Note*:** Computed from Primary Data

Here, the regression coefficient C' is less than C, and p- value indicates a significant difference. So, it can be concluded that the mediating variable mediates the relationship between dependent and independent variables. Since the indirect effect through the mediation variable is less than the direct effect. Burnout adversely affects the relation between the Psychosocial Work Environment and Turnover Intention. Since the p-value is significant, there is mediating effect.

Objective 4 sought to analyse the mediating effect of Job Burnout on the relationship between Psychosocial Work Environment and Turnover Intention. Results show that a Psychosocial Work Environment affects Turnover Intention through Job Burnout.

This study tested the direct and indirect (mediation through Job Burnout) effects of Psychosocial Work Environment on Turnover Intention. Based on the mediating model, Job Burnout mediates the negative effects of the Psychosocial Work Environment on Turnover Intention. The researcher acknowledges that the direct impact of the Psychosocial Work Environment on Turnover Intention has been observed, highlighting the mediating role of Job Burnout.

More specifically, the results suggest that the Job Burnout dimensions of Emotional Exhaustion, Mental Exhaustion and Physical Exhaustion are key factors in the increase of Turnover Intention among retail textile shop salespersons in Kerala. In addition, this study results show that the Psychosocial Work Environment is a significant positive predictor of Job Burnout, which corroborates previous research findings (Borritz et al.,2019). Moreover, previous research proposes that burnout has a mediating position between organisational factors influencing work conditions of employees and outcome variables such as job satisfaction, organisational commitment, turnover intentions, work performance, and health problems

Several studies support the hypothesis that psychosocial work environment aspects of salespersons' encompassing the nine areas of work-life directly impact feelings of burnout, especially Emotional, Mental and Physical Exhaustion. This study indicates that the Psychosocial Work Environment influences Turnover Intention through the partial mediation effect of Job Burnout. Again, this result indicates that Job Burnout indeed mediates some of the negative behaviours of employees. Increased job demand, abusive supervision job insecurity of salespersons tend to result in Emotional, Mental and Physical Exhaustion, triggering a rise in employee Turnover Intention. This observation merits serious attention from management and human resource departments from retail textile shop managers.

The result suggests that organisations are concerned about improving workers' mental health to reduce their job burnout syndrome from a practical standpoint.

4.19.5 Path Analysis

The Model fit indices (Table 4.50) show how well the model fits the set of relationship.

Figure 4.22

Integrated Model

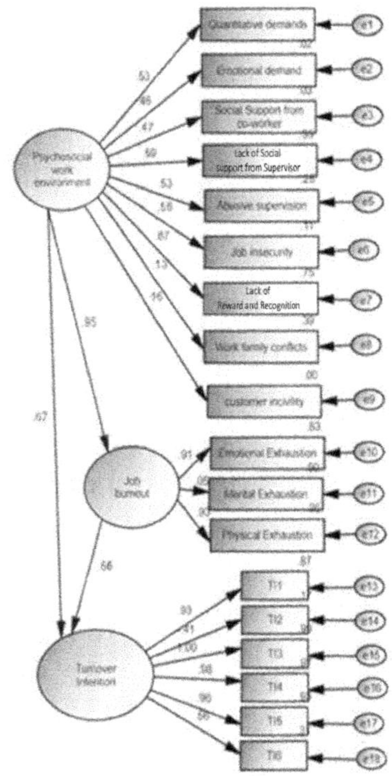

Table 4.51
Model fit Indices

	χ^2	DF	P	Normed χ^2	GFI	AGFI	NFI	TLI	CFI	RMSEA
Model	3.578	4	.000	4.634	.946	.538	.919	.914	.924	.074
Recommended Value	>0.05	<5	>0.05	<5	>0.9	>0.9	>0.9	>0.9	>0.9	<.08

***Note*:** Computed from Primary Data

From the table, it is very clear that the values for measurement variables are conforming with the recommended values. Hence, the model can be considered as a good fit model. All the attributes loaded significantly on the latent constructs. The value of the fit indices indicates a reasonable fit of the measurement model with data. After running the chi-square value, DF, GFI, AGFI, NFI, TLI, CFI, RMSEA. And it is often considered acceptable that shows close good model fitness level. Overall values for model fit indices and measures obtained in the study are at the acceptable level. Hence, it can be concluded that the proposed model is fit. In table 4.51shows the regression coefficients.

Table4.52

Integrated Relationship of the Study Variables

Regression Coefficients	Estimate	Critical Ratio (CR)	p-value
Psychosocial Work Environment → Turnover Intention	0.674	5.588	<0.001
Psychosocial Work Environment → Job Burnout	0.951	36.612	<0.001
Job Burnout → Turnover Intention	0.662	15.827	<0.001

***Note*:** Computed from Primary Data

Table 4.5 presented Regression weights of the integrated relationship between variables. From the value of the estimate shows that Psychosocial Work Environment (β = 0.274). Job Burnout (β= 0.951) and Turnover Intention (β=0.662) has significant influence on each other.

4.20 Chapter Summary

The plan of analysis is explained in detail in this chapter. In the first section, the researcher goes over the specifics of the respondents' demographic profiles. Following that, the data were checked for normality and reliability. Then, to evaluate the measurement model, Exploratory Factor Analysis and Confirmatory Factor Analysis (CFA) was performed. Later on, the conceptual research model was tested using the Structural Equation Modelling (SEM) technique. Following that, the relationship between the independent, dependent, and mediating variables was analysed and illustrated the integrated model. The findings, discussions, and conclusion are focused on in the next chapter.

CHAPTER 5

SUMMARY OF THE FINDINGS, SUGGESTIONS, AND CONCLUSION

This chapter deals with the data analysis results, findings, suggestions, implications, future scope, and conclusions. An overview of the study begins with a brief recapitulation of the research and then discusses the summary of the findings. The chapter ends by presenting the study's implications in its theoretical and practical perspectives. Finally, future research considerations and overall conclusions are provided.

5.1 Overview of the Study

The current research aims to understand the reliable predictors of Turnover Intention among salespersons in the retail textile shops in Kerala. The retail textile sector is significantly affected by various Psychosocial Work Environment issues, especially internal work stressors and Job Burnout. For example, many salespersons are affected by Physical Exhaustion due to the long working hours and prolonged standing. In addition, they are emotionally and mentally affected due to Abusive Supervision, Lack of Social Support from Co-workers, Improper Reward and Recognition as well as Job Insecurity. The study was based on primary data, collected through interview schedules from the selected salespersons. Empirical testing was done with the conceptual model developed based on a literature review. Data was collected from 398 salespersons from the retail textile shops in Kerala. The data analysis was carried out by employing appropriate statistical methods for drawing meaningful results and interpretation.

5.2 Findings based on the Demographic Profile of the Salespersons

This section deals with the study's major findings, which are organised into different subsections. The first section is devoted to the Demographic Profile of the Salespersons such as District, Circle, Gender, Age, Marital Status, Monthly Income, Working Hours, and Work Experience of the salespersons in the retail textile shops in Kerala.

5.2.1 District and Circle-wise Distribution of the Salespersons

As stated in the preceding chapter, the researcher recognised the districts with more salespersons from the three zones of Kerala state. They are Calicut from the northern zone, Ernakulam from the central zone, and Trivandrum from the Southern zone.

For administrative purposes, the labour department has divided each District into different circles based on the strength of the salespersons. Therefore, the researcher has chosen two circles among the three districts, each based on the highest number of salespersons.

Ernakulam district has the highest population of salespersons. This is because the number of retail textiles shops and the total number of salespersons working in the retail textile shop is more in Ernakulam.

5.2.2 Age and Gender of the Salespersons

The analysis indicates that more than half of salespersons belong to 20-30 years of age. Therefore, it shows that most salespersons working in retail textile shops are youngsters. Older people struggle to keep up with the pace of change in the industry and demand long working hours and prolonged standing. The retail textile sector requires emotional management and physical health throughout long working hours, so most salespersons come under the age group of 20- 30.

Furthermore, the dissemination of gender represents that 57 per cent are female, and the remaining 43 per cent are male.

5.2.3 Marital Status and Educational Qualification of the Salespersons

The study shows that the majority of salespersons are married. Married salespersons, especially women salespersons, are considered more for sales jobs as their best career option since they have a low educational background. Moreover, a fixed monthly income from this job helps them to take care of their family expenses and domestic responsibilities such as child care and home-related commitments.

In addition, 37.9 per cent of the salespersons hold a high school education. Furthermore, 20.4 per cent of salespersons are graduated. As retail sales jobs require less skill and educational background, privately-owned big retail salesperson positions usually require only high school level education. However, most branded retail textile employers prefer applicants with diplomas or degrees.

5.2.4 Work Experience and Monthly Income of the Salespersons

According to the study, 9.8 per cent of the salespersons have 15-20 years of experience, and 37.2 per cent have 1-5 years of experience.

It is clear from the study that 4 per cent of salespersons earn a monthly income above ₹ 20000, and 20.6 per cent of the salespersons earn a monthly income below ₹10000. And most salespersons are getting income between ₹10000 – 15000.

5.2.5 Working Hours per day of the Salespersons

The study found that most of the salespersons (49 per cent) work 11 - 12 hours per day.

5.3 Findings of the Study Objectives

This section is devoted to the study's findings in relation to the Objectives.

5.3.1 Objective 1: To Study the Effect of Psychosocial Work Environment on Turnover Intention

The Psychosocial Work Environment is measured by using variables like Quantitative Demand, Emotional Demand, Lack of Social Support from Supervisors, Social Support from Co-workers, Abusive Supervision, Job Insecurity, Lack of Reward and Recognition, Work-family Conflict, and Customer Incivility. The nine tested hypotheses findings are as follows.

5.3.2 Quantitative Demand and Turnover Intention

Quantitative Demand has a substantial positive influence on Turnover Intention. The study results show that salesperson devote more time to their jobs and work for longer (minimum12 hours each day). It is tough for them to maintain a high energy level throughout the day. Salespersons must stand for long periods due to the nature of their work. All weekends, national holidays, and festival seasons have a higher quantitative job demand. The frequent movement from counter to dispatch area from one customer to another is another quantitative demand for the salesperson.

Salespersons are responsible for checking the stock on the counter, ensuring that the display label matches the price of the goods, determining which items are selling well and which are not. Salespersons' responsibilities also include bringing things from the storeroom to the counter, displaying the products, reassembling the customer's disturbed goods, inspecting the goods, and keeping an eye on any suspicious customers. Then, when the store closes, they are still responsible for re-checking the physical stock of goods, cleaning the store, smoothing exhibited objects, and checking the trial room and other places to ensure the store is secure and no one has left and closing the counter.

Salespersons must become more vigilant in keeping an eye on the store to prevent loss and damage to merchandise. They must clean up display items more frequently in crowded retail environments. In addition, some days salesperson's working hours are increasing due to overcrowded shops.

5.3.3 Emotional Demand and Turnover Intention

Emotional Demand has a significant positive influence on Turnover Intention. As retail textile shop salespersons, they have to control their emotions in the workplace. A salesperson has no right to express their real feelings to customers or supervisors. If they do so, they may lose their job. Some salespersons also mentioned that sometimes they do not get time to go for lunch when they feel hungry, and whereas the customers are provided with the refreshments frequently.

5.3.4 Social Support from Co-worker and Turnover Intention

Social Support from Co-worker has a substantial negative influence on Turnover Intention.

Most of the salespersons in the retail textile shops get proper support from their co-workers. Most of them believe that their co-workers are supportive and ready to help and share their various job demands. Current study results also show that salespersons have enough social support from co-workers, not leading to turnover intention. However, few salespersons believe that sales targets create rivalry among Co-workers. On the contrary, these sales targets are beneficial for employers. Because it increases the sales volume and rivalry reduces cooperation among co-workers. So, in future, they will not come for any labour rights or collective bargaining.

5.3.5 Lack of Social Support from Supervisor and Turnover Intention

Lack of Social Support from supervisors has significant positive influences on Turnover Intention. Increased supporting behaviour, concern for the well-being of employees, and demonstrating respect to subordinates are all linked to supervisor support. However, most salespersons in Kerala's retail textile shops, particularly those owned by private individuals, said their supervisors did not provide enough assistance and recognition. Moreover, they do not feel valued. The salesperson from branded stores, on the other hand, said they were getting enough help, recognition, and respect. This is because supervisors are ready to listen to the salesperson's needs and develop great bonds with their salespersons.

5.3.6 Abusive Supervision and Turnover intention

Abusive Supervision has a significant positive influence on Turnover Intention. However, most supervisors are not professionally qualified in Kerala's retail textile sector. They are frequently unpleasant and disparaged towards salesperson in front of customers or co-workers. Punishments such as floor changes, section changes, and warehouse responsibilities are common among salespersons. However, these are not regarded as part of the job rotation and are instead considered a punishment. Some supervisors initiated disciplinary action against salespersons based on closed-circuit television (CCTV) footage, and these supervisors always monitor them through CCTV. If any salesperson takes a few minutes to relax, the supervisor will come and assign them to one or more duties. Salespersons have also stated that in some establishments, supervisors will not allow them to sit even if there are no customers to attend. According to some young salespersons, they sit on the floor as if they were cleaning the lowest rack of the shelf, or sometimes they sit under the display table, out of sight. Some supervisors are quite selective, and they have a preferred group of salespersons. Supervisors assign good customers to their favourite group of salespersons, and they quickly reach their sales targets, and others get fired. In some establishments, salespersons are fired if a customer does not make purchase. Hence, they are sometimes forced to beg the customer to make a purchase.

Usually, human beings thrive in communities, and when they share their feelings and emotions, they can work more effectively. However, the retail textile business creates an environment that does not allow for any informal ties to develop at the workplace. For example, salespersons are not permitted to go to lunch together or exchange their mobile phone numbers, nor they are allowed to attend any family occasions of their Co-workers. As a result, all of these factors significantly impact a salesperson's Intention to turnover.

Even though Abusive Supervision is prevalent in retail textile shops, some salespersons responded that their supervisors are very cooperative, democratic, and fair towards them.

5.3.7 Job Insecurity and Turnover Intention

Job Insecurity has a significant positive influence on Turnover Intention. According to salespersons, Job Security is substantially low in retail textile shops. As a result, if they make minor mistakes, they risk losing their jobs. For instance, employees are penalised in certain shops if they take five or seven days off or negatively react to a supervisor's hostile attitude. Simultaneously, certain other groups of salespersons think that their jobs are secure, except for fraudulent salespersons.

5.3.8 Lack of Reward and Recognition and Turnover Intention

Lack of Reward and Recognition has a significant positive influence on Turnover Intention. Most salespersons are not getting any promotion opportunities like floor managers or supervisors. No appreciation for the good efforts. Some other salespersons are said to be getting proper Rewards and Recognition. Their employer selects the best employee of the month and gives gifts and other promotional opportunities.

5.3.9 Work-Family Conflict and Turnover Intention

Work-Family Conflict has no significant influence on Turnover Intention. Salespersons always have to work at weekends and late evenings, festivals such as Onam, Christmas, Vishu, Eid, and public holidays. However, most of the salespersons responded that because of all these work-related constraints, those who have firm family support either from parents or from spouses can survive in this sector. Majority of salespersons have that support.

5.3.10 Customer Incivility and Turnover Intention

Customer Incivility has no significant influence on Turnover Intention. The intensity and frequency of customer incivility in the retail textile sector are very less. Moreover, most salespersons said, they like to interact with a customer, which is a stress relief and provides satisfaction to salespersons.

5.4 Objective 2: To study the effect of Psychosocial Work Environment on Job Burnout

The second objective is to study the effect of a Psychosocial Work Environment on Job Burnout. The findings are based on the nine tested hypotheses are given below.

5.4.1 Quantitative Demand and Job Burnout

Quantitative Demand has a significant influence on Job Burnout. There exists a significant positive influence. In the short term, high quantitative job demand may motivate the employees, but in the long term, it leads to stress and job burnout syndrome among salespersons.

5.4.2 Emotional Demand and Job Burnout

Emotional Demand has a substantial influence on Job Burnout. There exists a significant positive influence between Emotional Demand and Job Burnout. The prolonged existence of emotionally disturbing attitudes from superiors or high emotional demand is positively related to job burnout among salespersons. The demands and expectations of managers, colleagues, and customers are constantly changing, and salespersons in the retail industry may find themselves under a lot of pressure to keep up with the pace of change.

5.4.3 Social Support from Co-worker and Job Burnout

Social Support from Co-worker has a significant influence on Job Burnout. There exists a significant negative influence between Social Support from Co-worker and Job

Burnout. The study results revealed that Social Support from Co-worker help salespersons to reduce their burnout level through effective communication and cooperation with each other.

The cordial relationships with their co-workers have a tendency to foster feelings of trust and compassion among them, encouraging them to foster their peers' psychological and emotional well-being (Sloan, 2012; Halbesleben & Wheeler, 2012; McGuire, 2007). Finally, employees who get co-worker Support are more likely to develop a high sense of personal accomplishment through inspiration from their co-workers. Many studies in the occupational stress literature recognise that Social Support from Co-workers may be differently effective in reducing work-related stressors and Burnout.

5.4.4 Lack of Social Support from Supervisors and Job Burnout

Lack of Social Support from Supervisors has a substantial influence on Job Burnout. There exists a significant positive influence between Lack of Social Support from supervisors and Job Burnout. Some salespersons are of the opinion that they have high quantitative and emotional job demands and are not getting sufficient support and motivation from their supervisors. So due to this high job demand and low resources and low Social Support from the Supervisor they will experience Job Burnout.

5.4.5 Abusive Supervision and Job Burnout

Abusive Supervision has a substantial influence on Job Burnout. There exists a significant positive influence between Abusive Supervision and Job Burnout. Most of the salespersons responded that their supervisor's frequent hostile verbal and non-verbal behaviour includes being disrespectful while also being abusive and talking to others in an abusive tone. Long term presence of these dysfunctional interpersonal attitudes in the workplace tends to stress salespersons which progressively turn into job burnout.

5.4.6 Job Insecurity and Job Burnout

Job Insecurity has a substantial influence on Job Burnout. There exists a significant positive influence between Job Insecurity and Job Burnout. In some retail textile shops, Job Insecurity is very high. The salespersons from that shop responded that they are from a low social and economic background and do not have many job opportunities. So, becoming unemployed is traumatic for these salespersons and results in Job Burnout syndrome among salespersons.

5.4.7 Lack of Reward and Recognition and Job Burnout

Lack of Reward and Recognition has a substantial influence on Job Burnout and exists a significant positive influence between Lack of Reward and Recognition and Job Burnout. Some salespersons are of the opinion that they are not getting proper Rewards and Recognition in accordance with their physical and emotional strain. Salespersons of the retail textile shop with a lack of recognition and reward are more susceptible to Job burnout.

5.4.8 Work-Family Conflict and Job Burnout

Work-Family Conflict has no substantial influence on Job Burnout. Since most salespersons are of the opinion that they have enough family support, work-family conflict does not significantly influence Job Burnout.

5.4.9 Customer Incivility and Job Burnout

The result shows that Customer Incivility has no significant influence on salespersons' Job Burnout. Most salespersons are happy to interact with customers, and very few have a negative experience with customers.

5.5 Objective 3: To examine the effect of Job Burnout on Turnover Intention

The third objective is to study the effect of Job Burnout on Turnover Intention. The findings are based on the three tested hypotheses given below.

5.5.1 Emotional Exhaustion and Turnover Intention

Emotional Exhaustion has a substantial influence on Turnover Intention. There exists a significant positive influence. The prolonged existence of psychosocial risk factors in the retail textile shops leads to emotional resource depletion and emotional strain. So, gradually salesperson feels weak, used up, and unable to face daily hassles. It is also typical for the emotionally exhausted salespersons to experience a lack of energy to deal with their regular working duties and feeling tired gradually leads to a strong sense of turnover intention among salespersons.

5.5.2 Mental Exhaustion and Turnover Intention

Mental Exhaustion has a substantial influence on Turnover Intention. There exists a significant positive influence between Mental Exhaustion and Turnover Intention. Long term stress tends to Mental Exhaustion among salespersons and reduces the motivation and mindfulness of the salespersons to work in a particular shop where they work. Mental Exhaustion increases the negative attitude towards oneself, work and life itself. Feelings of detachment and apathy can cause chaos in employees' personal and work life. Employees may feel trapped in the workplace with no job control. Finally, it leads to a strong sense of turnover intention among salespersons.

5.5.3 Physical Exhaustion and Turnover Intention

Physical Exhaustion has a significant influence on Turnover Intention. There exists a significant positive influence between Physical Exhaustion and Turnover Intention. When a salesperson is emotionally and mentally disconnected from their work, high physical efforts like prolonged standing and demanding constant energy directly influence salespersons' Physical Exhaustion, such as low energy, tiredness, lack of focus, and muscle tension. Quantitative job demand directly connects with the Physical Exhaustion of salespersons. The inherent challenge that comes along with high job demands can help people thrive at their jobs, but it can also cause problems when workers are challenged too much, especially when this 'too much' lasts for an extended period of time, as has been shown in the literature.

5.6 Objective 4: To examine the mediating effect of Job Burnout on Psychosocial Work Environment and Turnover Intention

The fourth objective of the study is to examine the mediating effect of Job Burnout on the Psychosocial Work Environment and Turnover Intention.

This study tested the direct and indirect (mediation through job burnout) effects of Psychosocial Work Environment on Turnover Intention. Based on the mediating model, Job Burnout partially mediates the negative effects of the Psychosocial Work Environment on Turnover Intention. The researcher acknowledges that the direct impact of the Psychosocial Work Environment on Turnover Intention has been observed, highlighting the mediating role of Job Burnout.

5.7 Suggestions

According to various cross-sectional studies, psychosocial factors vary based on the nature of work or occupation. Blue-collar and white-collar jobs have different job stress profiles. Each type of industry, for example, manufacturing, health care work, retailing, and public administration, also has its own Psychosocial Work Environment profile. Therefore, depending on the type of occupation or industry Psychosocial Work Environment will also differ.

The researcher suggests three sides of the responsibilities to concentrate and reduce the Psychosocial Work Environment, Job Burnout, and Turnover Intention issues. One side is salespersons from the retail textile shop. They should be aware of the psychosocial health and safety conditions of the shops. Second is the responsibility of retail employers, who need to provide a conducive work environment. Next is the role of the supervisors in the retail textile shops. Finally, the researcher provides some general suggestions to government authorities and the labour department.

Based on the study's findings, the following suggestions are recommended to overcome the Psychosocial Work Environment risk factors, Job Burnout, and Turnover Intention problems among the retail textile salespersons.

5.7.1 Employers' Initiative for a Good Psychosocial Work Environment

The main criteria for a good Psychosocial Work Environment include work characteristics such as interpersonal relations, social support, role at work, feeling valued, and balance between various functions. One strategy to promote a good Psychosocial Work Environment in the retail textile shop is to encourage social support of the salesperson and participatory job design. But specific job stressors related to customer care cannot be avoided. However, this study report shows that the frequency and intensity of Customer Incivility are very low, which has no effect on Job Burnout and Turnover Intention among salespersons in retail textile shops.

5.7.1.1 Develop Internal Guidelines to Manage Psychosocial Risks

Dealing with psychosocial risk is more of a social design process than a technological one in the workplace. As a result, establish guidelines for a successful work (re)design process, which involves sophisticated collective problem-solving procedures and the creation of an atmosphere conducive to the development of successful organisational problem-solving processes.

- Establish a staff-management committee on preventing health and safety issues at work. Additionally, the employer should provide a counseling session once a month with an expert's help.
- Retail textile shops can control their internal social stressors by implementing a zero-tolerance policy against harassment or other humiliations against salespersons. In addition, provide training programmes for improving leadership practices for supervisors.
- Suggestion boxes can be placed in different accessible locations within the retail shop for anonymous complaints. So, it will be helpful for salespersons who have a fear to speak out openly.
- A routine direct observation from the management teams can be a great problem solver. However, frequent one-on-one conversations, group meetings, and salespersons counseling sessions are the best strategies.
- Periodic Rewards and Recognition can motivate salespersons to deal with their work and relationship with a retail shop. As a result, retailers can select the best employees and promote supervisors or floor managers.
- Retailers may increase salespersons' self-esteem by participating in the product selection process. In addition, if any salesperson has any skills related to fashion designing, retailers can send them for better training and employ the salesperson's skills.
- Festival celebrations, a slight warm-up session in the morning, and playing light music on the floor also helps to reduce burnout level. Organisation sponsored picnics can also help salespersons take a break from the daily stressors associated with work.

- To avoid constant movement of the salespersons from counter to dispatch session with one customer to another customer, retailers can install conveyors in their shops so salespersons can avoid physical fatigue due to constant stair climbing.
- To reduce the physical strain on the salespersons due to prolonged standing, retailers should provide a sit-stand chair, a chair or stool would be provided for the worker, so they should sit down at regular intervals. Use of good shoes and floor mats to avoid standing on a hard surface and footrests are also helpful to reduce the strain on the backbone.
- Implement workplace health risk management, including hazard identification, risk measurement, and preventive interventions. Allow increased social interactions and collaborative action in times of conflict.
- Redesign work culture and personnel management to attract, recruit and maintain the salespersons' well-being and satisfaction.

5.7.2 Supervisors in the Retail Textile Shop

- Supervisors themselves are focused on encouraging positive behaviour for the benefit of the retail establishment they supervise.
- Always keep fair treatment within the retail shop. Fair treatment includes justice at work and respect, which helps to keep salespersons retention.
- If a salesperson goes through a stressful conversation with a customer or other person, provide a few breaks to relax.

5.7.3 Salespersons' Self-Regulation

- If a salesperson is stressed, he or she can access support from friends, family, and co-workers.
- Increasing coping skills like proper diet, proper sleep, and learning deep relaxation to better manage job stressors.
- Using pioneering relaxation techniques such as yoga and pranayama to manage their burnout level.
- Starting an open discussion with the supervisor helps to come out from the burnout phase.

5.8 General Suggestions

5.8.1Government Interventions to Prevent Psychosocial Risks

India's Occupational Health and Safety services are still in the preliminary stages. In Europe and some other developed countries, psychosocial risks in the workplace represent a constant priority. It helps them reduce the frequency of psychosocial risks to a great extent. However, in India, regulatory mechanisms and related guidelines on mental health at work and the management of psychosocial risks are still lacking (Work, 2008).In addition, due to a lack of policy development with psychosocial risks and work-related stress, it is difficult for organisations of all sizes to implement successful control strategies to deal with these issues. This shortage aggravates India's occupational health and safety issues in the retail textile sector. The researcher suggests a few remedial measures that government authorities can carry forward.

5.8.1.1 Regulatory Mechanism

- Implement new policies and regulations by amending the Shops and Commercial Establishment Act. Add more provisions to protect the psychosocial well-being of the salespersons in the retail textile shops. A substantial proportion of "soft" policy initiatives should be relevant to protect emotional and mental health to reduce psychosocial risks in the workplace. Take the initiative to mobilise policymakers, organisations, and individual salespersons.
- Existing Occupational Health and Safety (OHS) legislation in India should focus more on the issues related to workplace psychosocial hazards. Implement strict policy regulation against Abusive Supervision, high Emotional and Quantitative Job Demands, and other work-related stressors.
- Additionally, the national government can seek the assistance of research institutes to develop a range of initiatives addressing these issues, ranging from scientific research to guidelines, tools, training, and awareness-raising activities.

5.8.1.2 Labour Officers

- Labour officers can effectively enforce all laws and regulations concerning health and safety at retail textile shops. In addition, they can encourage textile retailers to ensure occupational safety and health management systems are efficiently established in their shops to improve workplace safety and health.
- The labour officers can conduct a mandatory awareness camp for the salespersons about psychosocial risks and legal remedies and provide participation certificates. Only those with this certificate can work as a salesperson.
- Labour officers can also conduct training programmes for supervisors regarding effective employee management to enhance the psychosocial well-being of salespersons.
- The labour inspectorate and social partners can provide guidance. The concerned ministry can develop a helpline number to assist salespersons with their work-related complaints, which specialised inspectors should staff.
- Employers were provided with a brief guidance document summarising the requirements and advising to manage psychosocial risks in the workplace.

5.9 Theoretical Implication

From a theoretical point of view, the study adds to the existing literature and helps extend the frontiers of knowledge in occupational health and safety. It provides a framework to researchers and academicians to explore more psychosocial factors that are significant in the retail textile sector in India. Overall findings contribute to further understanding of the cross-cultural aspects of reliable predictors of employee psychosocial health in collectivist societies.

5.10 Practical Implication

Apart from the theoretical application, the research findings have specific practical considerations. The results indicate that the psychosocial factors primary influence the salespersons' turnover intention in the retail textile shop work environment.

Retail managers can use the findings of this study to reduce the psychosocial risk factors, job burnout syndrome, and turnover intention among salespersons. Specifically, the management of the retail shop should be committed to establishing and maintaining psychosocial support, which helps salespersons cope with problems arising from Emotional, Mental and Physical Exhaustion because psychosocial support increases salespersons sense of competence and identity. However, employing mentors appears to create additional costs for the firm. With this realisation, the retail textile shop management can benefit from senior salespersons as potential mentors for professional assistance to junior salespersons. Furthermore, retailers can hire salespersons with family support to avoid work-family conflicts.

The present study includes direct and indirect (mediating effect of Job Burnout) effects of Psychosocial Work Environment on Turnover Intention among salespersons. The result has shown that Job Burnout and Turnover Intention among salespersons in retail textile shops are related to Psychosocial Work Environment risk factors.

There is a great practical need to assess psychosocial factors at work and improve salespersons' well-being. For example, poor working conditions and burnout employees are affected by sickness absence, occupational accidents, poor performance, and reduced productivity. In contrast, the opposite is true for good working conditions and employee engagement. So ultimately, psychosocial factors and salespersons' well-being translate into financial business outcomes. Therefore, it is in the enlightened self-interest to regularly monitor psychosocial factors at work and employees' well-being so that timely and targeted measures can be taken to prevent burnout and reduce turnover intention.

The result of this study is useful for retailers since it has a number of practical applications for handling employees' burnout in the workplace. Moreover, they can also identify the major psychosocial risk factors they must avoid in their work environment. With the help of this study's conceptual framework, retail managers can implement essential leverage points that could be possible to improve the well-being of the salespersons. Practically, this study report can help retailers to design to reduce unreasonable quantitative and emotional job demands such as excessive physical effort, unsupportive supervisors, and rivalry among co-workers. It can also help improve job resources such as appropriate rewards, recognition, and performance feedback. For instance, salespersons might be assisted to meet job demands and attain their personal and organisational goals. Importantly, these practices are not necessarily expensive to the retailers.

Supervisors can be more supportive by reducing the employee's workload, clarifying role-related expectations, providing timely and appropriate performance feedback, and ensuring that the employee feels valued as a salesperson. In doing so, salespersons would not feel unsatisfied, strained and inefficacious professionally. Thus, the less they suffer from job burnout, the lesser the Intention to leave the shop. Redesign work culture and improve personnel management to attract, recruit and maintain the well-being and satisfaction of the salespersons.

When it comes to salespersons, a work environment can be created that encourages the positive growth of energy, vigour, participation, commitment, absorption, and efficiency.

Supervisors get more insights into the importance of improving their Supervision. In addition, it will help them to offer adequate, constructive feedback and establish a cordial atmosphere in the workplace.

5.11 Future Scope of the Study

This study can further extend to other retail segments where employees face similar health problems. Psychosocial Work Environments may differ depending upon the nature of the work environment. The light can be thrown on other sectors like railways, hospitals, and education institutions to understand the psychosocial health problems of the employees, and outcomes like performance, commitment, and coping strategies can be provided based on the nature of the industry.

While this study was considered more relevant to retail textile shops, various other factors are also seen in the existing literature that was not included in the study. Therefore, future researchers should look for opportunities to collect data investigating those factors under a similar framework. For instance, the role of factors like employee engagement and organisational commitment may be explored as mediators in future studies.

Researchers can also investigate the effect of the Psychosocial Work Environment on the salesperson's personality traits and demographic characteristics.

Not many studies have been done in the Indian context, so it applies to different sectors to understand the employees' Psychosocial Work Environment issues and well-being. Furthermore, researchers can study other consequences of a Psychosocial Work Environments like depression how it affects job performance, job commitment and absenteeism.

Future researchers can consider ergonomic design within the retail workplace to help reduce the physical strain and stress of the salesperson.

Future research focusing more on the salespersons' ability to cope with Emotional, Mental and Physical Exhaustion will be practically helpful for suggesting modifications in the recruitment and selection process to alleviate this serious problem. In addition, a mixed-method approach like quantitative and qualitative analysis gives more insights into the concepts.

5.12 Conclusion

The common phenomenon of any industry or organisation is to maximise profit through labour and machine. The retail industry is one of the fastest-growing industries and one of India's second-largest employment providers.

There is ample evidence that organisational vitality is not possible without individual vitality - our major challenge is to make organisational management aware of this connection.

The study showed that poor psychosocial working conditions are connected to an increased risk of Job Burnout and Turnover Intention among salespersons. Actions to improve employee satisfaction may be a promising path in preventing work-related psychosocial health problems. However, more studies are needed to disentangle causal pathways between specific psychosocial work environment exposures and employee risk factors.

In summary, this is one of the first studies to examine the effect of the Psychosocial Work Environment on Job Burnout and The Intention to Leave among salespersons in the retail textile shops in Kerala. So, as part of the occupational health psychology literature, this study adds to it by providing empirical evidence about psychosocial risk factors that contribute to Job Burnout and Intention to Leave among salespersons.

9 781805 251392

Printed by BoD™ in Norderstedt, Germany